Careers in Focus

TRAVEL & HOSPITALITY

THIRD EDITION

Ferguson
An imprint of Infobase Publishing

Careers in Focus: Travel & Hospitality, Third Edition

Copyright © 2007 by Infobase Publishing

Ferguson
An imprint of Infobase Publishing
132 West 31st Street
New York NY 10001

Library of Congress Cataloging-in-Publication Data

Careers in focus. Travel & hospitality. — 3rd ed.
  p. cm.
 Includes bibliographical references and index.
 ISBN 0-8160-6590-X (hc: alk. paper)
 1. Hospitality industry—Vocational guidance—Juvenile literature. 2. Tourism—Vocational guidance—Juvenile literature. I. J.G. Ferguson Publishing Company. II. Title: Travel & hospitality.

 TX911.3.V62C39 2007
 647.94'023—dc22

Ferguson books are available at special discounts when purchased in bulk quantities for businesses, associations, institutions, or sales promotions. Please call our Special Sales Department in New York at (212) 967-8800 or (800) 322-8755.

You can find Ferguson on the World Wide Web at http://www.fergpubco.com

Text design by David Strelecky

Printed in the United States of America

MP MSRF 10 9 8 7 6 5 4 3

This book is printed on acid-free paper.

Table of Contents

Introduction

There are four basic necessities of travel: transportation, lodging, dining, and entertainment. When planning a trip, most travelers first gather information on these four elements by checking the current availability and cost of transportation, lodging, and food at their planned destination.

Many travelers find it easier to let a professional help with the information gathering and planning. In such cases, travelers consult a travel agency. The goal of travel agents working for a travel agency is to help their clients plan a trip that meets their desires and fits within their travel budget. Specifically, they check rates on transportation and accommodations and make transportation and hotel reservations. Agents also provide information such as visa and medical requirements for travel abroad, and they supply additional directions specific to the traveler's needs.

There is another option for travelers that simplifies the planning process even more: the packaged tour. Packaged tours, which can range from several days to several weeks, are available for those who wish to have many aspects of a trip planned in advance. They may cover a number of countries or they may include just one city the entire time. Tourists have a wide variety of tours to choose from to meet their specific needs and interests. Travel agencies, private groups, museums, universities, and other institutions are just some of the organizations that provide packaged tours.

One specific type of packaged tour is adventure travel, which has become one of the fastest-growing segments of the travel industry. This type of travel is geared toward the more physically active traveler who enjoys both seeing and exploring great wonders. Adrenaline-pumping activities such as kayaking, whitewater rafting, and hiking are just some of the pursuits available to the adventure traveler. Hundreds of outfitters make a living organizing and guiding such trips, which may include a weeklong trip sea-kayaking in Baja or whitewater rafting in the Grand Canyon. Outfitters usually specialize in one sport, but some of the bigger companies take on several sports. Outfttters usually take groups of eight or more people on their trips.

For tourists interested in spending much of the time actually moving from one point to another, cruise ships provide a slower, more leisurely type of travel. Cruises provide enough entertainment that some passengers regard them as floating vacation spas. Some of the most popular cruises today are to the Caribbean and Alaska.

There are seven main branches of the lodging, or hospitality, industry. Front office, service, marketing and sales, and accounting and financial management make up the "front of house" positions, or those most visible to the public. Less visible "back of house" jobs include food and beverage, housekeeping, and engineering and maintenance. Most branches of this industry operate on a three-shift system, allowing for 24-hour service for hotel guests.

The front office deals with all the paper and computer work involved with room and reservation assignments. The people working in this department also run the reservation desk, switchboard, and mail room. A general manager heads this department, as well as the entire hotel operation and employees. Department supervisors report to the general manager.

The main purpose of the service branch is to make the guests feel welcome. This includes greeting guests, parking cars, running the elevators, opening doors, carrying baggage, preparing rooms, and assisting with travel plans and entertainment. Most jobs in this department require little training or further education, thus creating a great starting place for people eager to break into the lodging industry.

The accounting and financial management branch controls the fiscal affairs of the hotel. Projects such as financial policy and planning and maintenance of records and statements, overseeing expenditures, bank accounts, and payroll are some of the ninny responsibilities of this department. Many of the accounting executives rise to leading hotel positions.

The marketing and sales sector strives to attract potential customers. The employees of this department try to find out what guests want in a hotel. Marketing and sales workers often use surveys, focus groups, or other research methods to gauge the feelings and opinions of guests and potential guests.

The food and beverage departments are among the largest and most lucrative sectors in the hospitality industry. They include all the services involved with the bars and restaurants of a hotel, as well as room service, from purchasing to food preparation and presentation.

Depending on the size of the hotel, the housekeeping department can easily number in the hundreds. The room and floor attendants are responsible for keeping the rooms clean and supplied with fresh linens and towels. Executive housekeepers oversee the workers in the housekeeping department.

The engineering and maintenance departments keep the facilities of a hotel, motel, or other establishment in working order. The responsibilities include plumbing, painting, electrical wiring, and general repairing. They also help the housekeeping staff with the heavier tasks of keeping a hotel clean.

Travel and hospitality is one of the largest retail service industries in the United States. Total 2005 expenditures for domestic and international travelers in the United States were more than $646 billion, according to the Travel Industry Association. This represents an increase of 5 percent from 2004.

There is a growing trend toward more frequent, shorter vacations. Three- and four-day weekends are replacing the two-week vacations that were common in previous decades. Since people in the United States work more and are hard-pressed for time to take long vacations, many travel organizations have designed their programs around shorter trips.

Another trend is the growth in adventure travel and ecotourism, which involves visiting a pristine natural area, learning about its ecosystem, perhaps even performing some environmentally helpful work while there, and making every effort to preserve and protect that ecosystem without altering it by the act of traveling there. Ecotours to such places as the Galapagos Islands and Costa Rica have become very popular. Public interest in environmental issues is likely to encourage this trend in the future, although travelers may choose domestic rather than foreign destinations.

The positive outlook for the travel and tourism industry took a sudden turn after the terrorist attacks of September 11, 2001. The threat of more terrorism has affected consumer confidence and corporate travel policies. Air transport and corporate and convention travel were particularly hard hit. Foreign travel to the United States was also been affected. However, the steady increase in foreign and domestic travel over the past several years indicates that people are regaining confidence and looking for new destinations. This bodes well for many of the career in the travel and hospitality industry.

Each article in *Careers in Focus: Travel & Hospitality* discusses a particular occupation in detail. Most articles appear in Ferguson's *Encyclopedia of Careers and Vocational Guidance* but have been updated and revised with the latest information from the U.S. Department of Labor and other sources.

The **Quick Facts** section provides a brief summary of the career including recommended school subjects, personal skills, work environment, minimum educational requirements, salary ranges, certification or licensing requirements, and employment outlook.

This section also provides acronyms and identification numbers for the following government classification indexes: the *Dictionary of Occupational Titles* (DOT), the *Guide for Occupational Exploration* (GOE), the National Occupational Classification (NOC) index, and the Occupational Information Network (O*NET)-Standard Occupational Classification System (SOC) index. The DOT, GOE, and O*NET-SOC indexes have been created by the U.S. government; the NOC index is Canada's career classification system. Readers can use the identification numbers listed in the Quick Facts section to access further information about a career. Print editions of the DOT (*Dictionary of Occupational Titles*. Indianapolis, Ind.: JIST Works, 1991) and GOE (*The Guide for Occupational Exploration*. 3d ed. Indianapolis, Ind.: JIST Works, 2001) are available at libraries. Electronic versions of the NOC (http://www23.hrdc-drhc.gc.ca) and O*NET-SOC (http://online.onetcenter.org) are available on the World Wide Web. When no DOT, GOE, NOC, or O*NET-SOC numbers are present, this means that the U.S. Department of Labor or Human Resources Development Canada have not created a numerical designation for this career. In this instance, you will see the acronym "N/A," or not available.

The **Overview** section is a brief introductory description of the duties and responsibilities involved in this career. Oftentimes, a career may have a variety of job titles. When this is the case, alternative career titles are presented.

The **History** section describes the history of the particular job as it relates to the overall development of its industry or field.

The Job describes the primary and secondary duties of the job.

Requirements discusses high school and postsecondary education and training requirements, any certification or licensing that is necessary, and other personal requirements for success in the job.

Exploring offers suggestions on how to gain experience in or knowledge of the particular job before making a firm educational and financial commitment. The focus is on what can be done while still in high school (or in the early years of college) to gain a better understanding of the job.

The **Employers** section gives an overview of typical places of employment for the job.

Starting Out discusses the best ways to land that first job, be it through the college placement office, newspaper ads, or personal contact.

The **Advancement** section describes what kind of career path to expect from the job and how to get there.

Earnings lists salary ranges and describes the typical fringe benefits.

The **Work Environment** section describes the typical surroundings and conditions of employment—whether indoors or outdoors, noisy or quiet, social or independent. Also discussed are typical hours worked, any seasonal fluctuations, and the stresses and strains of the job.

The **Outlook** section summarizes the job in terms of the general economy and industry projections. For the most part, Outlook information is obtained from the U.S. Bureau of Labor Statistics and is supplemented by information taken from professional associations. Job growth terms follow those used in the *Occupational Outlook Handbook*. Growth described as "much faster than the average" means an increase of 36 percent or more. Growth described as "faster than the average" means an increase of 21 to 35 percent. Growth described as "about as fast as the average" means an increase of 10 to 20 percent. Growth described as "more slowly than the average" means an increase of 3 to 9 percent. Growth described as "little or no change" means an increase of 0 to 2 percent. "Decline" means a decrease of 1 percent or more. Each article ends with **For More Information**, which lists organizations that provide information on training, education, internships, scholarships, and job placement.

This revised edition of *Careers in Focus: Travel & Hospitality* also includes photos, sidebars, and interviews with professionals in the field.

Adventure Travel Specialists

OVERVIEW

Adventure travel specialists develop, plan, and lead people on tours of places and activities that are unfamiliar to them. Most adventure travel trips involve physical participation and/or a form of environmental education. A whitewater rafting trip, a mountain climbing expedition, or a safari are just some examples of adventure travel. Organized adventure travel has grown rapidly in popularity over the past few decades, and today it represents a segment of the travel industry generating more than $166 billion per year in the United States alone.

HISTORY

Adventure travel as a formalized activity began developing in the late 20th century. As Americans enjoyed an increasingly high standard of living, as the advancement of technologies made everyday life easier (or "softer"), and as disposable incomes grew, some people began to see vacations as not simply a time for relaxation but for adventure. What distinguishes adventure travel from traditional activities such as camping in the great outdoors? Some experts maintain that those involved in adventure travel are deliberately seeking some type of risk in or an unknown outcome for the activity.

Mountain Travel, founded in 1969, and Sobek, founded in 1973, became two of the leading adventure travel companies in the United States, merging in 1991 as Mountain Travel Sobek. Today

QUICK FACTS

School Subjects
Business
Foreign language
Geography

Personal Skills
Helping/teaching
Leadership/management

Work Environment
Primarily outdoors
Primarily multiple locations

Minimum Education Level
Some postsecondary training

Salary Range
$16,840 to $28,090 to
$60,000+

Certification or Licensing
Required for certain
positions

Outlook
About as fast as the average

DOT
353

GOE
11.02.01

NOC
N/A

O*NET-SOC
39-6021.00

adventure travel is one of the fastest growing areas of specialization within the travel industry. Specialists escort paying customers to destinations all over the world—China, Nepal, Easter Island, Alaska, to name a few—and organize activities such as mountain climbing, sea kayaking, and camel-back desert crossings. The adventure travel industry looks to continue its growth in the 21st century. Some experts note that this is in part due to the computer and the Internet: As more and more people spend workdays sitting in cubicles facing computers, more and more feel distanced from fulfilling physical activities and real feelings of excitement. At the same time, the Internet, with its breadth of information, has made the world a smaller place and given people greater knowledge of travel destinations and possibilities.

THE JOB

Adventure travel specialists plan—and may lead—tours of unusual, exotic, remote, or wilderness locations. Almost all adventure travel involves some physical activity that takes place outdoors. Adventure travel is split into two categories: hard adventure and soft adventure. Hard adventure requires a fairly high degree of commitment from participants, as well as advanced skills. A high-adventure traveler might choose to climb Yosemite's El Capitan, raft the Talkeetna River in Alaska, or mountain-bike the logging trails in the Columbia River Gorge. Soft adventure travel, on the other hand, requires much less physical ability and is usually suitable for families. Examples of this kind of travel might be a guided horseback ride through the Rocky Mountains, a Costa Rican wildlife-viewing tour, or a hot air balloon ride over Napa Valley, California.

Steve Gilroy is a professional photographer who has turned his love of the Alaskan outdoors into a second career—that of "soft adventure" travel specialist and guide for photography tours. Each year, his company, Alaska Photo Tours, takes approximately 120 photography buffs on tours of the Alaskan countryside, allowing them to capture spectacular scenery and wildlife on film.

"We offer custom trips for small groups that put people into great photographic situations," he says. "It's for people who like taking pictures and who don't want to be caught in a huge tour group or be in the really touristy places." Gilroy's trips originate in either Anchorage or Juneau and last seven to 12 days. His tour groups are small, with no more than 11 travelers. He plans every detail of each of the company's 12 yearly trips, and he serves as a guide on about half of them.

Some adventure travel specialists work strictly in an office environment, planning trip itineraries, making reservations for transportation, activities, and lodging, and selling the tours to travelers. Others, typically called *outfitters*, work in the field, overseeing the travelers and guiding the tour activities. In some cases, such as Gilroy's, the adventure specialist both plans the logistics of the trip and guides it.

For every adventure tour that takes place, numerous plans must be made. Travelers who purchase a tour package expect to have every arrangement handled for them, from the time they arrive in the city where the trip begins. That means that ground transportation (such as vans, buses, or jeeps), accommodations (lodges, hotels, or camping sites), and dining (whether hiring cooks and arranging for food to be taken on the trip or finding appropriate restaurants) must all be planned and reserved, all depending upon the particular trip. Each day's activities must also be planned in advance, and arrangements must be made with adventure outfitters to supply equipment and guides.

Gilroy begins planning a trip more than 18 months in advance. With attention to every detail, he plans tours that will take travelers to the right places at the right times of the year for the best photographic opportunities. "We dictate the schedule around the wildlife and the scenery," he says. "I only travel at the best times." Long before the tour ever begins, he has reserved lodging, any in-state flights, natural history guides for certain locations, and even private rooms in restaurants.

Some companies serve as adventure travel brokers, selling both tours that they have developed and tours that have already been packaged by another company. Travel specialists working for brokers are responsible for marketing and selling these tours. They give potential customers information about the trips offered, usually over the phone. When a customer decides to purchase a tour package, the travel specialist takes the reservation and completes any necessary paperwork. Depending on their position in the company and their level of responsibility, adventure travel planners may decide where and how to advertise their tours.

Working as an adventure travel outfitter or guide is very different from working as an adventure travel planner or broker. The duties for these individuals vary enormously, depending upon the types of tours they lead. Adventure tours can take place on land, on water, or in the air. On a land adventure trip, guides may take their tour groups rock climbing, caving, mountain biking, wilderness hiking, horseback riding, or wildlife viewing. On a water trip, they may go snorkeling, scuba diving, surfing, kayaking, whitewater rafting, or canoeing. Air adventures include skydiving, parasailing, hang gliding, bungee jumping, and hot air ballooning.

Whatever the nature of the trip, guides are responsible for overseeing the group members' activities. For Gilroy, this starts at the beginning of a tour when he collects his travelers from the airport. He then conducts an orientation meeting and discusses the coming days' activities. "I give them a plan of attack and tell them what the next day's goals are," he says. "I'll say, 'We're hoping to see whales tomorrow . . . or we're going to see if we can get a bald eagle to swoop down by the boat.' I try to give them some expectation of what we might see."

Gilroy's tours usually consist of a segment in coastal Alaska, one near Mount McKinley, and one in his hometown of Talkeetna to give travelers a taste of life in rural Alaska. "Most visitors want a balanced trip," he says. "So this way, they get to see the glaciers, sea otters, whales, and puffins of coastal Alaska, plus the grandeur of Mount McKinley and the grizzlies, caribou, moose, wolves, and tundra." The tour group usually spends between three and five days in each location.

Tour guides are also responsible for demonstrating activities, helping with equipment, and assisting group members who are having difficulty. In many cases, where travelers are interested in the scenery, geography, wildlife, or the history of a location, guides serve as commentators, explaining the unique aspects of the region as the group travels.

As the tour guide, Gilroy's objective is to take his groups out into the Alaska landscape to look for photographic opportunities. When touring on land, they travel in a 15-passenger luxury van, which makes periodic stops at likely locations. "We take short hikes, with vehicle support," he says. "We'll stop, gather our equipment, and go for a short walk because I know of good photo opportunities in the area, or we've spotted an animal." During each of the visitors' hikes, Gilroy educates them on their surroundings. "As we walk, I give them background on the wildlife, what to look for, how to approach," he says. "It's important to me to share the whole Alaska experience . . . vegetation, wildlife, natural history."

Guides are also responsible for helping tour group members in the case of an emergency or unforeseen developments. Depending on the nature of their tour, they must be prepared to deal with injuries, dangerous situations, and unusual and unplanned happenings. In Gilroy's case, this means advising group members on how to stay safe in the unfamiliar territory. "I always tell them what to be careful of," he says. "I tell them about bear behaviors, how to walk on the lumpy tundra so that they don't twist an ankle, that sort of thing." All of the guides on Gilroy's tours are required to be trained in first aid and CPR.

Adventure tours are meant to be unique experiences. One way guides make their trips special is to provide their clients with unusual access to the environment or "up close and personal" experiences. Gilroy, for example, often contracts with a local flight service company to take his groups on aerial tours of Mount McKinley. Some tours also include short cruises off the coast in Zodiacs, or motorized rubber skiffs. "This allows us to go ashore, to walk a beach littered with car-sized icebergs, to go into a meadow where the wildflowers are gorgeous," Gilroy says. The goal is a photographic exploration of Alaska.

No matter what the theme of a trip is or its destination, it is the guide's responsibility to ensure that tour group members have a safe, memorable, and enjoyable time.

REQUIREMENTS
High School
If you are considering the business end of travel—working in a brokerage, planning tours, or eventually owning your own tour-packaging business—you should start taking business courses while still in high school. Accounting, computer science, mathematics, or any other business-related course will give you a good start. Classes in geography, geology, social studies, and history might also help you understand and discuss the locations you may be dealing with. It is important to take a foreign language, a study you will probably need to continue throughout your career. Finally, classes in English or speech are always good choices for helping you develop the ability and confidence to deal with people.

If you are more interested in the fieldwork aspect of adventure travel, you will need to take classes that help you understand how the earth's environment and ecosystem work. Because tour guides often explain the natural history of a location or educate tour groups on local wildlife and plant life, classes in earth science, biology, and geology are excellent choices. Classes that teach you about the social history of various places, such as social studies or anthropology, might also be beneficial.

Postsecondary Training
There are several different approaches you can take to prepare for a career in adventure travel. While it may not be necessary for all

jobs, a college degree will likely give you a competitive edge in most employment situations. If you choose to obtain a college degree, some options for majors might be earth science, biology, geology, natural history, or environmental affairs. If you hope to become involved with an intensely physical form of adventure travel, a degree in health, physical education, or recreation may be a good choice.

If you are more interested in the planning and reservations end of adventure travel, a college degree in business is a good choice. Some adventure travel brokers suggest that attending one of the many travel agent schools also provides a good background for the administrative aspects of the business.

It may be possible to find a job in adventure travel without college training, if you happen to be very experienced and skilled in some form of adventure activity. If you choose this path, you should spend as much time as possible developing whatever skill interests you. There are classes, clubs, and groups that can teach you anything from beginning diving to advanced rock climbing.

Certification or Licensing

The Institute of Certified Travel Agents offers the designations certified travel associate (CTA) and certified travel counselor (CTC) to agents with the appropriate education and experience. While such certification is not required, it may be helpful to those running their own travel businesses.

Many employers do require employees to have certification in certain areas, such as CPR and first aid. Also, depending on the job, you may need special certification or licensing, such as scuba certification so that you can lead diving activities, or licensing as a commercial driver so that you can transport clients in a company van or other vehicle. If you plan to open your own adventure tour operation, you will need to apply for a business license. Check with your local government offices for details on how to obtain one.

Other Requirements

"People who enter this career are the kind of people who just naturally spend their free time outdoors," says Steve Gilroy. "So, they grew up hiking and fishing and camping . . . and that love of outdoors just carried them to the point where they decided to combine their love of nature with their career." Adventure travel tour guides need to have a passion for sharing their love of nature and their knowledge with others. Also, because of the nature of this job, you should be in good physical shape. Other important qualities to have are maturity, responsibility, and common sense, especially when leading groups of travelers into the relative unknown. Some employers may have minimum age requirements for those in certain positions.

Adventure travel professionals who work in an office, developing and selling tours, need some different personal qualities than those who work in the field. Dave Wiggins, who owns one of the nation's oldest adventure travel brokerages, says that he looks for people with a good work ethic. "You can train someone to do everything else, but you can't teach the right attitude." Wiggins says that it's also important to be friendly and confident, and to have good phone skills. "We look for people with a good head on their shoulders who can speak intelligently about the different programs we sell," he says. While being an active, outdoorsy person may help you sell tours, it is not a requirement for working in this branch of adventure travel. Attention to detail and good organizational skills are more significant.

The 10 Commandments for Ecotourism

1. Respect the frailty of the earth.

2. Leave only footprints. Take only photographs. No graffiti! No litter!

3. To make your travels more meaningful, educate yourself about the geography, customs, manners, and cultures of the region you visit.

4. Respect the privacy and dignity of others. Ask first before snapping a picture.

5. Do not buy products made from endangered plants or animals.

6. Always follow designated trails.

7. Learn about and support conservation programs.

8. Whenever possible, walk or use environmentally sound methods of transportation.

9. Patronize businesses that advance energy and environmental conservation.

10. Encourage organizations to subscribe to environmental guidelines.

Source: American Society of Travel Agents

EXPLORING

Since much adventure travel involves physical activity, which may range from low to high impact, taking courses or becoming involved in activities that promote physical fitness is a good idea. If you already have an interest in a particular activity, you may be able to join clubs or take classes that help you develop your skills. For example, scuba diving, sailing, hiking, mountain biking, canoeing, and fishing are all activities found in adventure travel that you might be able to engage in while still in high school.

Another way to explore this field is to go on an adventure outing yourself. Outward Bound USA, for example, offers a wide variety of programs for teenagers, college students, and adults. And don't forget to check out summer camp options. YMCA camps, scouting camps, and others provide the opportunity to learn about the outdoors and improve your camping skills. Summer camps are also excellent places to gain hands-on experience as a worker, whether you are a counselor, a cook, or an activity instructor.

EMPLOYERS

Commercial adventure travel agencies, naturally, are employers of adventure travel specialists. In addition, a number of not-for-profit organizations, such as universities and environmental groups, are also offering nature and adventure programs.

STARTING OUT

Make a list of adventure groups and do some research. How long have they been in business? Do they specialize in soft or hard adventure travel? You can narrow your search to companies that specialize in the activity or activities with which you have experience. Use the Internet to help you do this; many companies have websites that advertise their specialties and list job openings. Other organizations, such as The International Ecotourism Society, also provide information on jobs and internships at their websites. Remember that for your best chance of finding a job in adventure travel, you may have to relocate, so your search should be geographically broad.

There are a number of magazines that may be helpful in compiling a list of companies involved in adventure travel. Some good publications to look into are *Outside* (http://www.outsidemag.com), *Backpacker* (http://www.backpacker.com), and *Bicycling* (http://www.bicycling.com). A final method of getting a list of travel wholesalers and outfitters is to contact one or all of the adventure travel organizations listed at the end of this article. These associations should be able to give you a list of their members.

To find not-for-profit organizations that hire adventure travel specialists, consider the National Audubon Society and the Sierra Club. Check with your local library for a complete listing of environmental groups. You might also contact universities to see if they have a wilderness/adventure travel division in their schools of physical education or recreation.

You should also use any contacts you have—from clubs, organizations, previous travel experiences, or college classes—to find out about possible employment opportunities. If you belong to a diving or bicycling club, for example, be sure to ask other members or instructors if they are familiar with any outfitters you could contact. If you have dealt with outfitters in some of your adventure trips, you might contact them for potential job leads.

ADVANCEMENT

There is no clearly defined career path for adventure travel specialists. For those who work in an office environment, advancement will likely take the form of increased responsibility and higher pay. Assuming a managerial role or moving on to a larger company are other advancement possibilities.

For those who work in the field, advancement might mean taking more trips per year. Adventure travel in many locations is seasonal, and therefore, tour guides may not be able to do this sort of work year-round. It is not uncommon for an individual to guide tours only part time, and have another job to fill in the slow times. For those who become experienced in two or more particular areas of travel and develop a reputation of expertise, however, there may be the opportunity to spend more, or even all, of the year doing adventure touring.

Another option for either the office worker or the guide would be to learn about the other side of the business. With experience in all aspects of developing, selling, and leading tours, ambitious travel specialists may be able to own their company. "You could become your own tour operator in an area that you know and love," says Steve Gilroy, "which is what I've done."

EARNINGS

There is very little information available on what adventure travel specialists earn. Those who work in the field may find that they have peak and slack times of the year that correspond to destination weather conditions or vacation and travel seasons. Specialists, especially those just starting out in this line of work, may find they need to work two or three seasonal jobs in different locations and for different employers in order to have work throughout the year. As specialists gain experience, it may be possible for them to find year-round work with one employer, and, of course, many experienced travel specialists also have the goal of starting their own business and working for themselves. Experience, employer, and amount of work done are all factors that influence earnings per year.

According to the U.S. Department of Labor, travel guides of all types had median yearly incomes of $28,090 in 2004. The lowest paid 10 percent made less than $16,840 per year, while the highest paid 10 percent earned more than $46,510.

Adventure travel specialists who work in the field generally receive free meals and accommodations while on tour, and they often receive a set amount of money per day to cover other expenses. Major tour packagers and outfitters may offer their employees a fringe benefits package, including sick pay, health insurance, and pension plans.

WORK ENVIRONMENT

Depending on where they work, an average day for adventure travel specialists might be anything from planning tours in the comfort of an air-conditioned office to leading a safari through southern Africa. Tour planners may do the majority of their work in comfortable offices. However, they need to spend some time in the field to better plan adventure tours. How can they recommend an activity without knowing the ins and outs?

For those who find cruising TV channels more appealing than rafting down the Colorado River or observing wildlife, this is definitely the wrong career choice. Adventure travel involves a great deal of physical activity. Tour guides are always on the go, whether guiding a group up and down a formation of rocks, or keeping an eye out for lichen-eating caribou.

Adventure specialists work with groups. In some cases, operators schedule up to 40 tourists per trip. Longer trips may require step-on operators, or local specialized guides, who give tours lasting one day or longer. In such cases, it helps to be able to work well with others. Communication is an important buzzword in this industry.

OUTLOOK

In 2004, tourism reached an all time high of 763 million international travelers, according to the World Tourism Organization. A large percentage of all international tourists embark on nature- and wildlife-related trips. This indicates that the market for adventure travel is quite large.

Many trends in today's society indicate that this growth is likely to continue. One reason is that the public's awareness of and interest in physical health is growing; this leads more and more people to pursue physical activities as a form of recreation. Another reason is that as more people realize that a healthy environment means a better quality of life, there is an increased interest in wildlife and wilderness issues. Adventure travel often encompasses both physical activity and education on and preservation of natural areas, so it is a natural choice for many travelers.

Despite the general growth in the field, however, it should be noted that jobs as tour guides may not be easy to come by. Compared to the rest of the travel market, the adventure segment is still fairly small. Perhaps more significantly, tour guide positions are considered very desirable. According to Dave Wiggins, job openings for fieldwork in adventure travel are somewhat limited and highly sought after. "There are outfitters out there who get maybe 500 applications a year," he says. "And they can hire maybe two new people."

FOR MORE INFORMATION

For information on careers, training in niche travel, and travel news, contact
American Society of Travel Agents
1101 King Street, Suite 200
Alexandria, VA 22314
Tel: 703-739-2782
Email: askasta@astahq.com
http://www.astanet.com

For information on certification and continuing education for travel agents, contact
The Travel Institute
148 Linden Street, Suite 305
Wellesley, MA 02482
Tel: 800-542-4282
Email: info@icta.com
http://www.icta.com

For information on the ecotourism industry and related careers, contact
International Ecotourism Society
1333 H Street, NW, Suite 300, East Tower
Washington, DC 20005
Tel: 202-347-9203
Email: ecomail@ecotourism.org
http://www.ecotourism.org

Visit the OIA website for the latest press releases and adventure travel news.
Outdoor Industry Association (OIA)
4909 Pearl East Circle, Suite 200
Boulder, CO 80301
Tel: 303-444-3353
Email: info@outdoorindustry.org
http://www.outdoorindustry.org

For statistical information and industry news, contact
World Tourism Organization (WTO)
Capitán Haya 42
28020 Madrid, Spain
Email: omt@world-tourism.org
http://www.world-tourism.org

Visit the Cool Works website for information on seasonal job opportunities in national parks, resorts, cruise ships, and more.
Cool Works
http://www.coolworks.com

Visit the Outward Bound USA website to learn more about its adventure activities.
Outward Bound USA
http://www.outwardbound.org

Amusement Park Workers

OVERVIEW

Amusement park workers function in a variety of jobs. Some are employed to construct, maintain, and operate thrill rides; others, assigned to the front gate, issue tickets or passes; some work concession stands or manage park restaurants and gift shops; many are employed as entertainers. There are also numerous behind-the-scenes departments such as security, marketing, or personnel. Each particular department, regardless of the amount of customer contact, is necessary for the smooth and profitable operation of the park, as well as the enjoyment of the park patron.

HISTORY

Amusement parks, most often located at the end of a trolley line, were built as attractions to stimulate weekend ridership on trolley cars. The early amusement parks consisted of picnic grounds, dance halls, restaurants, and a few games and simple rides.

The World's Columbian Exposition held in Chicago, Illinois, in 1893, had a huge impact on the industry. The Expo featured the Ferris Wheel, a huge mechanical ride, that was the hit of the fair. The Ferris Wheel is still a staple in many parks today. One of the biggest innovations of the Expo was the introduction of the midway concept. By arranging gaming booths, concession stands, and rides on either side of a walkway, people had to pass every attraction to get from one end of the park to the other.

After enjoying success with his Water Chutes park in Chicago, Paul Boynton was inspired to establish another facility at the existing Coney Island resort in New York City in 1895. Many people came to visit the two-mile boardwalk and beach for the attractions, carnival games, and shows. For the next 30 years, Coney Island was a popular amusement park and served as a model for the many other parks opening throughout the United States. By 1919, there were over 1,500 amusement parks in operation. Coney Island remains a popular New York tourist attraction today.

In the 1930s and early 1940s, the Great Depression and the onset of World War II almost destroyed the industry. The poor economy and forced rationing of supplies closed many parks. Indeed, by 1939, only 400 amusement parks were still open. The industry received a boost with the post-war baby boom. Many parks, using a new concept, the Kiddieland, pulled in a new generation of park goers with family-oriented attractions and rides.

By far, the most successful pioneer of the amusement park industry was Walt Disney. He opened Disneyland in 1955, using themes as the basis of the park layout and concept, instead of traditional rides and concessions. Disneyland offered the public, or "guests," five different theme lands and times, such as Tom Sawyer's Island, Futureland, and Cinderella's Castle, for a fixed price. Disneyland was, and still is, hugely successful, and it has become the springboard for future Disney parks—Disney World, Epcot Center, and Tokyo Disneyland.

Many companies have tried to duplicate Disney's achievements. One of the most successful has been the Six Flags company. Six Flags now has 29 theme parks throughout the United States, specializing in thrill rides, variety shows, and music concerts. Another popular park is Cedar Point, in Sandusky, Ohio.

A day at an amusement park remains a popular family activity. However, in order to keep fresh and attract repeat customers, parks are constantly adding new rides and more elaborate shows and parades, in essence reinventing themselves to suit the public's ever-changing tastes and attitudes.

THE JOB

Amusement parks employ a variety of workers to run their parks smoothly and efficiently. Of course, the number of employees depends on the size of the park, its attractions, and whether or not the park is open year-round.

The Ferris Wheel

What amusement park is complete without the Ferris Wheel? This famous ride was invented in 1893 by George Washington Gale Ferris for the World's Columbian Exposition held in Chicago, Illinois. It stood 264 feet high and had 36 pendulum cars that could hold 60 passengers each, for a total of 2,160 passengers. About one dozen steel companies were contracted to work on the wheel due to its immense size—1,200 tons. Though the wheel's price tag was steep, about $350,000 (in 1893), it was such a popular ride with the public that the manufacturing cost was recovered in a few weeks' time.

Equipment maintenance and operation is one of the industry's largest departments. *Ride operators* work the control panel by monitoring the speed of the ride, accelerating or slowing down to load and unload passengers. Some operators are responsible for light maintenance of the rides—paint touch-ups, replacing light bulbs or other decorations, and refueling engines.

Ride attendants collect fares or tickets. They help passengers get on the rides and make sure they are safely fastened or locked in before the ride begins. Attendants are also responsible for lining up waiting groups of people in a quiet and orderly manner.

Some amusement parks have water-themed attractions such as the water logs or boat rides. Special attendants stationed at such rides make sure passengers load the water vehicles correctly and instruct them on certain rules for a safe and enjoyable trip.

Attendants may also be stationed at fun houses, haunted houses, or the hall of mirrors. Such attendants operate the special effects machinery and make sure patrons walk through the attraction in an orderly and timely manner.

Pony rides, petting zoos, and pig races are common attractions at amusement parks and carnivals. *Animal handlers* are needed to feed and care for the animals. They also help passengers mount the ponies, give children food to feed the animals, and match children who wish to ride with appropriately sized animals.

There are many kinds of concession stands at amusement parks, each one staffed by one or more attendants. Game booths are big draws at an amusement park. Games of chance using balls, milk jugs, water, rings, and bottles are just some examples of different booths. *Game attendants,* also called *concessionaires,* urge passersby to play, sell tickets, and maintain equipment needed to play.

They also reward winners with prizes such as stuffed animals, candy, or small trinkets.

Some amusement parks sell ticket packages ranging from one to several days. The cost of the ticket covers all rides, shows, and attractions. *Ticket attendants* sell tickets at a booth or counter located at the entrance of the park. Their duties include calculating the amount of tickets sold, making change, and processing credit card transactions.

What's a day at the park without food and drink? Amusement parks offer range of food—healthy and otherwise. *Food concession attendants* sell hot dogs, pizza, chips, popcorn, ice cream, cotton candy, lemonade, and beer, among other choices. The majority of these booths are located outside, though some attendants are stationed at indoor eateries. Food attendants are trained on the proper way to prepare and serve their snacks and make cash and credit card transactions as well.

Gift shop attendants work inside gift shops and also at outdoor souvenir booths. Besides making and completing cash and credit card sales, attendants are responsible for stocking and pricing items, helping customers with their purchases, and answering any questions regarding the merchandise. Attendants also make sure displays are clean and orderly.

The performance arts are favorite attractions at amusement parks. Many *singers, dancers, musicians,* and other *performers* are hired at the larger parks every year. Parades, comedy shows, and musical revues are just some examples of the entertainment provided at parks. Performers and *artists* are also needed to staff drawing and photo booths, fortune-telling tents, and other attractions.

The grounds crew is a important department no amusement park can do without. They are present throughout the day, though the bulk of their work takes place after hours. Maintenance and cleaning crews tidy the concession areas, ride platforms, and common walkways. They sanitize and resupply bathrooms and picnic areas. *Security workers* roam the park during operating hours and are responsible for maintaining order. *Parking attendants* sell parking tickets and usher cars into the proper parking spaces. They are sometimes called to help families with many children, or patrons with special needs. Some of the larger parks offer transportation from the parking lot to the main park entrance. At such facilities, employees are hired to drive trolley cars, trams, or trains and give general assistance to passengers.

No park can survive without a strong business department. *General managers* oversee operations of all park departments and employees. *Department managers* are responsible for the activity of their division and the work of their employees. They make weekly work schedules, train new employees, and address any complaints of the department. *Public relations specialists* are responsible for sending press releases to newspapers and other media sources to advertise an upcoming concert, new attraction, or the reopening of the park after a seasonal closure. *Human resource consultants* manage park personnel, including such tasks as deciding on new hires and arranging an orientation program for these employees. The human resource department is also responsible for organizing and managing the internship program.

REQUIREMENTS
High School
Most larger amusement parks require their employees to be at least 16 years old. Many high school students work at amusement parks every summer as a way to supplement their income while in school. If you want to stand out from the other applicants, consider taking classes such as mathematics, if you want to work ticket booths, gift shops, or anyplace where calculating and giving correct change is important; mechanics or industrial arts, if you want to work and maintain thrill rides; or speech and theater, if you want to be a performer. Unless you bear an uncanny resemblance to Bugs Bunny or Goofy, then it will be helpful to know how to dance and sing!

Postsecondary Training
Training for entry-level jobs such as a ride operator, game booth attendant, or fast-food worker consists of on-the-job training lasting about a week or two. Most parks train their employees on the particulars of the job, park rules and regulations, and grooming and behavior guidelines.

Most companies prefer college-educated individuals for their management positions. Consider majors in recreation, business management, or marketing (or performance art, if you want to be involved with the entertainment side of the business).

Other Requirements
People go to amusement parks for fun and excitement. Employees, because they have such contact with the patrons, should always be courteous, enthusiastic, and friendly. When dealing with the public, patience is key. The ability to communicate well is important when explaining game rules or park regulations—over and over and over.

There are many employment opportunities available for workers with physical challenges. Some examples include traditional positions in the business office—accounting, personnel, and marketing. A ticket booth can be adapted to accommodate an employee that uses a wheel-chair. It is best to contact each amusement park and check out their policies on such matters. Also, get in touch with your school counseling center, state office of vocational rehabilitation, or state department of labor for guidelines.

EXPLORING

Before you commit yourself to a lifelong career as an amusement park worker, why not spend some time exploring the field? Here are some suggestions:

Read up on the industry. An afternoon at the library or bookstore can educate you on the history, dynamics, and future of the amusement park industry.

Contact different amusement parks or their parent companies for research materials. Most public relations departments would be more than happy to send you press kits featuring park history, themes, and current attractions.

Spend some time at a local amusement park to get an idea of the different jobs available. (You'll have to convince your parents this is really for educational purposes!)

Does your school have a job shadowing program? Why not arrange to spend a day tagging along with different amusement park workers? You'll not only see the ins and outs of the industry, but you'll experience how hard these employees work. If you don't have access to such a program, consult with your school counselors about starting one.

Good news! Amusement parks hire high school students, age 16 or older, for many of their entry-level jobs. What better way to get a feel for the industry than spending a summer ushering kids onto the carousel ride, cajoling people to play the ring toss, or twirling together the biggest cotton candy cone in the world?

Volunteer to be a bingo caller. This will help you hone skills needed to be a good game attendant or even a carnival barker. Some places to try would be a neighborhood senior center, park district, or your local church.

EMPLOYERS

Since amusement parks are located nationwide, jobs can be found in almost every state. Note that most jobs are seasonal—usually from April to October. The larger parks do maintain some employees year-round, mostly those working in the business departments. In fact, the winter months are usually the busiest time for amusement parks. Advertising, funding, recruiting, company organization, new construction, and other prep work takes place during the off-season.

Only a few parks are open year-round, and these are located in warmer climates. Disneyland and Knotts Berry Farm, located in southern California, as well as Disney World and Busch Gardens, in Orlando, Florida, employ thousands of workers to run their parks.

Rarer still are indoor amusement parks. Some enclosed employment opportunities can be found at the Camp Snoopy amusement park located inside Minnesota's Mall of America.

STARTING OUT

Many amusement parks recruit at college campuses and job fairs; others visit local high schools. When attending such recruiting events, make sure your resume is up to date, and, if you're lucky, be ready for on-the-spot interviews. According to Scott Kirn, public relations specialist for Six Flags Great America in Gurnee, Illinois, the park hires about 3,000 full-time workers for the season, many of whom are high school and college students, as well as a growing number of senior citizens. Interns account for about 100 to 200 positions a year. "We look for people who are enthusiastic and entertaining, as well as hard working," Kirn says.

Technology plays a big part in today's job search process. The Walt Disney Company, for example, is increasing its reliance on online resume submissions. Its website (http://www.disney.com/DisneyCareers) offers a wealth of employment information such as job postings and their requirements, audition schedules, resume tips, and internship info. Any other questions? Click onto Disney's Q&A for answers to your job-related inquiries.

Whichever method you choose to apply for employment, it helps to be organized. First, contact your school placement center or the local library for a list of amusement parks in the area—or nationwide, if relocation is not a problem. Mail or electronically submit your resume/application to those that pique your interest. Follow up on your leads. Trade magazines such as *Amusement Business* (http://www.amusementbusiness.com), or organizations such as The International Association of Amusement Parks and Attractions (see For More Information), can be helpful in narrowing your job search. Some may even post employment or internship opportunities.

ADVANCEMENT

Advancement in this industry depends on the job. With work experience, a food and beverage cart attendant can be promoted to work at a park restaurant or snack shop and eventually become a restaurant manager. Employees with an interest in mechanics can start as an assistant in the mechanical department repairing and maintaining the rides and work their way to a supervisory position. A member of the chorus or dance troupe, after proper training and performing experience, can strive to be a principal dancer or one of Disney's character singers.

Interns stand an excellent opportunity for advancement. The time spent working on an internship brings valuable on-site work experience. Many companies may prefer to hire their former interns because they already know the company and the work involved. Knowledge and skills learned at amusement park jobs can easily be transferred to other fields such as hospitality or other areas of the entertainment industry.

Workers who aspire to work in a management position must understand that such jobs come with hard work and time served in the industry. College degree holders—in marketing, business management, hospitality, or related majors—will have the best chances at landing a management position.

EARNINGS

Though many entry-level amusement park employees earn minimum wage or slightly higher, weekly salaries will vary depending on the type and size of facility and its location. (Most amusement parks choose not to divulge salary information due to confidentiality reasons, though they do offer wages competitive with similar industries.) A recent survey conducted by the International Association of Amusement Parks and Attractions reports that front-line managers earn from $10,000 to $50,000, middle managers average about $44,000, and general managers averaged about $64,000. The U.S. Department of Labor reports that recreation workers of all types made a median annual salary of $19,320 in 2004. The lowest paid 10 percent made less than $13,260, while the highest paid 10 percent made more than $34,280.

All employees, regardless of work status, are given free admission to their park, as well as discounts for food and merchandise. If a certain theme is needed for a ride or concession, parks usually will provide the proper uniform free of charge. Some facilities also reward employees with family tickets and employees-only nights at the park.

Full-time employees receive a standard benefits package consisting of paid vacation, sick time, and health insurance. Some parks may offer relocation assistance.

WORK ENVIRONMENT

Attendants who work for traveling carnivals must move from town to town, usually every week or two. Some employees are housed in trailers or in motels. Relocation is necessary, of course, when applying for employment, or an internship, at parks in other cities. One Chicago area amusement park houses seasonal help at a nearby college.

Attendants assigned to work a ride, game booth, or concession cart must work in all kinds of weather; most parks do not close for anything but the most severe of storms. Workers assigned to gift shops or restaurants usually have clean and comfortable indoor work spaces. Performers and entertainers work both indoors and out, depending on the stage they are assigned to. They must sometimes perform in heavy theatrical makeup and bulky costumes, which can be uncomfortable in hot summer weather. Most employees work alone; ride attendants may work in pairs or assigned in teams.

Most amusement park employees work about 40 hours a week. Amusement parks are open every day during the season, so be prepared to work weekends and holidays—traditionally the busiest and most crowded times of the year. Parks may be open as late as 10:00 P.M.

OUTLOOK

According to the U.S. Department of Labor, employment of recreation workers should grow about as fast as the average through 2012. Most jobs will be for seasonal full-time work. Six Flags Great America, for example, hires more than 3,000 employees during the spring and summer months, though only 100 employees work year-round. Because the summer months are usually the busiest season at most U.S. amusement parks, employers compete to hire high school and college students who are on break from school. Most job opportunities will result from seasonal openings or current workers leaving the workforce. New construction of amusement parks is limited due to lack of funding, available land, and markets large enough to support such a project.

Though many people use their employment at amusement parks as a way to earn extra money during school, a number do take advantage of such jobs as a stepping-stone to a full-time career. If this appeals to you, consider a college degree in recreation, business management, or hospitality to help advance your goal. Do you have a knack for mechanics? Then look into work building, maintaining, and even designing roller coasters and other thrill rides. Many performers use their amusement park experience to build a career in the entertainment industry.

FOR MORE INFORMATION

For information on the industry and job opportunities, contact
International Association of Amusement Parks and Attractions
1448 Duke Street
Alexandria, VA 22314
Tel: 703-836-4800
Email: iaapa@iaapa.org
http://www.iaapa.org

For information on the history of amusement parks and attractions, industry publications, conventions, and membership information, contact
National Amusement Park Historical Association
PO Box 83
Mt. Prospect, IL 60056
http://www.napha.org

For a list of amusement and theme parks in the United States, or for historical facts on the industry, contact
FunGuide
http://www.funguide.com

For information on career and internship opportunities, contact
Six Flags Theme Parks
http://www.sixflags.com/Jobs

For career information, employment opportunities, or audition schedules, or to submit a resume electronically, contact
The Walt Disney Company
http://www.disney.com/DisneyCareers

Baggage Porters and Bellhops

OVERVIEW

Baggage porters and *bellhops*, known at some hotels as *uniformed service attendants, bell attendants,* or *guest services attendants,* are considered front-of-the-house jobs in the hotel industry. They are responsible for carrying guests' luggage to their room upon arrival and back to the lobby when they depart. At times they may be asked to run errands or deliver items for guests. Though bellhops work from the bell-stand—a desk or podium located in the hotel lobby—their work takes them all over the hotel property. Bellhops are also employed at airports, bus terminals, train stations, and just about any place of travel. There are about 54,310 baggage porters and bellhops employed in the United States.

HISTORY

Early in the hotel industry, the inn-keepers—the hotel owners and their immediate families—were responsible for every aspect of running a hotel. Besides working the front desk, cleaning the rooms, and cooking the food, they also had to carry guests' trunks and bags. As the industry grew, inn-keepers, many of whom had more than one hotel to manage, found themselves in need of reliable employees. The bellhop occupation grew from the idea of ultimate guest service. Many of the larger luxurious hotels have numerous bellhops in their bellstand department.

Bellhops and baggage porters are found in other areas of the travel and tourism industry as well. They work at transportation terminals such as airports, train stations, and cruise ships. In the late 1800s, the Pullman trains hired men, many of whom were African Americans, to work as porters for their first class sleeper cars. Referred to as Pullman porters, they were famous for the fine service and attention they gave to the first class passengers. The early Pullman porters had to abide by a strict behavior and work code and were highly respected members of the community. In time, Pullman porters became somewhat a symbol of black subservience, and the career became less popular.

THE JOB

Edward Wilson, a uniformed service attendant at the Hotel Intercontinental, Chicago, Illinois, starts his eight-hour shift at 7:00 A.M. There's no time for chatting or even a morning cup of coffee because a long morning of early checkouts and storage requests is about to begin. "We're really busy from about seven to nine in the morning," says Wilson. Guests who need to store their luggage until a flight later in the day can have the bellstand place their belongings in the storage area, more commonly known as the back closet. After guests are given claim tickets for each piece of luggage, the bags are stored according to size and weight. There is a late morning slow period before the crunch of the afternoon arrivals and check-ins.

All attendants are taught the proper way to carry a bag, especially the heavy ones, so as not to injure themselves. Many times guests will have questions about the room services, the hotel property, or the area surrounding the hotel. If Wilson or the other attendants cannot readily help, they direct the guests to the proper department. Sometimes Wilson is asked to deliver packages, mail, or faxes to guests or to run errands for them. If the hotel is particularly busy, he may help in other departments. Depending on the hotel, attendants may be asked to assist guests with disabilities, deliver ice or other supplies, provide directions to area attractions, or even drive the hotel van.

Tips are not mandatory, though hotel guests often give them in appreciation for good service. Attendants are allowed to keep the tips they receive, as compared to other industries where tips are pooled and divided equally among each employee. At the Hotel Intercontinental, Wilson and the other attendants are sent out in rotation. This method is fair and leaves working for big tippers to the "luck of the draw."

Much of Wilson's job relates to how well he deals with people— hotel guests and his coworkers. He views his fellow attendants as

Baggage porters and bellhops must be courteous and attentive to hotel guests' needs at all times. *(Getty Images)*

members of a team. "If I'm having a hard day at work," he says, "I can always count on the guys to crack a joke, cheer me up, and get me going again."

REQUIREMENTS

High School

There is no educational requirement for this position, though many hotels will insist that you have a high school diploma or a GED equivalent. Classes that will help prepare you for this work include any that will hone your people and communications skills as well as classes that will make you physically fit. Therefore, you should take English and speech classes, any business classes that focus on customer relations, and physical education classes. Edward Wilson credits his high school speech class in particular in helping him deal with the large and diverse groups of guests at the hotel. You may also benefit from taking basic math classes, local history courses, and geography. Bell attendants are often asked for information about the area or directions to special attractions, so you will do well to know as much as you can about the location surrounding the hotel where you work.

Certification or Licensing

Certification is not mandatory for this position. The most significant source of instruction for most bellhops is on-the-job training that may last up to one month. "At the Hotel Intercontinental, we had a week-long training program," says Wilson. "We were taught the correct way to handle bags and how to store them properly according to their weight class."

If certification does interest you, the Educational Institute of the American Hotel and Lodging Association offers training and certification classes for bellhops and baggage porters and other members of uniformed service. If you aspire to manage the bellstand someday or move to other departments in the hotel industry, you might want to consider certification.

Other Requirements

What makes a successful bellhop? Wilson says, "You should have good character and a friendly personality." Since bell attendants are often one of the first hotel employees with whom a guest interacts, it's important for them to make a good impression. This is a very people-oriented job. Even the most difficult guests must be served in an amiable and efficient manner. An outgoing personality and a desire to meet people from all over the country and world are good traits to have.

EMPLOYERS

Some of the smaller and simpler motels do not offer services such as those provided by bellhops. Most larger hotels, however, will often employ more than one bellhop per shift. This is especially true for large hotels located in busy urban areas, near airports, and hotels know for their luxury atmosphere. Other places of employment are Amtrak train stations, where porters, sometimes known as *red caps,* provide baggage help and airports, where those who help customers with bags may be known as *skycaps.*

STARTING OUT

Edward Wilson found his job through a church-sponsored job search program. He was looking to change careers when he came across a job description for the Hotel Intercontinental bellstand department.

Other methods for finding similar jobs include job fairs, job placement centers, newspaper want ads, and the Internet. Large hotels with websites often include postings of job openings, and a number of job agencies deal specifically with placing those interested in hospitality jobs (for example, visit the Web site http://www.hospitalityonline.com). Don't forget the old-fashioned way of job hunting: hit the pavement. Apply directly to the hotel's human resources department.

ADVANCEMENT

With enough work experience, go-getters can advance to the position of *bell captain*. Bell captains supervise the bellstand, give assignments to the bellhops, and take calls. Most hotels employ two bell captains, one each for the day and night shifts. Another position for advancement is that of *bellstand manager*. Considered the head of the department, bellstand managers are responsible for making work schedules, assigning extra staff when forecasts are heavy, and resolving any service problems.

EARNINGS

Most bell attendants are paid at an hourly rate, which may range from $5.93 per hour for the lowest 10 percent (making a yearly income of $12,334 for full-time work) to as high as $19.23 per hour (roughly $40,000 a year) for the highest 10 percent. The median salary is $8.69 an hour, or $18,075 per year. Bellhops are often paid the minimum wage, which varies by state, and in some cases is higher than the federal minimum. Bell attendants' total earnings are greatly supplemented with tips, which may add $100 a week or more to the income. A common rule for tipping bellhops is about $1 to $2 per piece of luggage. At some large, busy hotels bellhops may earn up to $100 a day in tips alone.

Full-time employees are offered health insurance, sick and vacation time, and employee discounts. Some hotels give discounted room rates for their employees.

WORK ENVIRONMENT

Their work takes bellhops all over the hotel property. They may be asked to unload luggage from a taxi and deliver it to a sleeping room, then be sent to a store to pick up a guest's special request. When the hotel is at full capacity, bellhops may be asked to help other departments, such as the concierge, mail department, or business center.

At larger hotels, there is usually more than one bellhop per shift. If checking in big groups or a guest with an extraordinarily large amount of luggage, attendants may be asked to work in pairs, so it helps to be a team player. Edward Wilson especially likes the camaraderie with the other attendants.

OUTLOOK

According to the U.S. Department of Labor, this field is expected to grow about as fast as the average through 2012. Employment in the hospitality industry, however, is greatly influenced by economic conditions, national events, and international events. During times of recession, fewer people spend money traveling for pleasure and businesses cut back on travel expenditures for employees. Additionally, events such as the terrorist attacks of September 2001 have a powerful, adverse effect on this industry. And since future attacks are unpredictable, the threat of terrorism will remain a destabilizing factor for the employment outlook of those in the industry. In addition to these negative factors on employment for bell attendants, many motels and smaller hotels increasingly are offering discounted sleeping rooms but very little service. Guests are expected to locate their rooms and carry their luggage. Some travelers, especially those on limited budgets, prefer to stay at these types of establishments. If this trend continues, there will be fewer jobs available for bellhops.

Nevertheless, job openings will be created as workers leave due to retirement, job transfers, or for other reasons. Bellhops often have a high turnover rate. Large hotels and those focusing on customer comfort will always have a need for the bellstand department and bellhops. Part of a four-star hotel's appeal rests in the sense of luxury and guest service provided. Bellhops and baggage porters at such lodging establishments are as much an expectation as they are a necessity. Baggage porters will continue to work at other travel venues such as the train or bus depot. Baggage service at airports, also known as skycap service, is also popular.

FOR MORE INFORMATION

For industry and career development information, contact
American Hotel and Lodging Association
1201 New York Avenue, NW, Suite 600
Washington, DC 20005-3931
Tel: 202-289-3100

Email: informationcenter@ahla.com
http://www.ahla.com

For information regarding training and certification, contact
American Hotel and Lodging Association Educational Institute
800 North Magnolia Avenue, Suite 1800
Orlando, FL 32803
Tel: 800-752-4567
http://www.ei-ahla.org

Bartenders

OVERVIEW

Bartenders mix and dispense alcoholic and nonalcoholic drinks in hotels, restaurants, cocktail lounges, and taverns. Besides mixing ingredients to prepare cocktails and other drinks, they serve wine and beer, collect payment from customers, order supplies, and arrange displays of bar stock and glassware. Bartenders, or their assistants, may also prepare fruit for garnishes, serve simple appetizers, replenish chips and pretzels, wash glasses, and clean the bar area. Approximately 474,000 bartenders work in the United States.

HISTORY

Tending bar was only one of the duties of the traditional innkeeper. When inns and small hotels were a family affair, and the drinks dispensed were no more complicated than a tankard of ale or a mug of mulled wine, bartending specialists were not required. Most recipes, such as rum punch, were commonly known; indeed, alcoholic beverages were more commonly drunk (and, because of dubious standards of public hygiene, safer) than nonalcoholic ones. However, beginning in the nineteenth century, the temperance movement helped to limit the acceptability of the widespread imbibing of distilled spirits. Drinking certain liquors in certain ways became a luxury and a fashionable statement, and the cocktail glass became the mark of the sophisticate. The trend towards increasing refinement of alcoholic beverages was only increased by the admittance of respectable women to bars, pubs, taverns, and saloons, and before long, everything from the absinthe frappe to the Manhattan had made its appearance. The number of recipes has only grown since; not even Prohibition could not stop the emerging science of mixology, as the all too often foul taste of the bootleg "bathtub gin" of the 1920s was not uncommonly disguised by elaborate recipes. Today, even in the average neighborhood cocktail lounge or tavern, they may have to cope with requests for such exotic concoctions as Screaming Zombies, Harvey Wallbangers, Golden Cadillacs, Singapore Slings, and hundreds of new recipes for shot drinks, or "shooters," complicated by the multiplicity of brands and flavors of liquor, beer, and "alco-pops."

THE JOB

Bartenders take orders from waiters for customers seated in the restaurant or lounge; they also take orders from customers seated at the bar. They mix drinks by combining exactly the right proportion of liquor, wines, mixers, and other ingredients. In order to work efficiently, bartenders must know dozens of drink recipes off the top of their heads. They should also be able to measure accurately by sight in order to prepare drinks quickly, even during the busiest periods. They may be asked to mix drinks to suit a customer's taste, and they also serve beer, wine, and nonalcoholic beverages.

A well-stocked bar has dozens of types and brands of liquors and wines, as well as beer, soft drinks, soda and tonic water, fruits and fruit juices, and cream. Bartenders are responsible for maintaining this inventory and ordering supplies before they run out. They arrange bottles and glassware in attractive displays and often wash the glassware. In some of these duties they may be assisted by *bartender assistants,* also known as *bar backs.*

Bartenders are responsible for collecting payment on all drinks that are not served by the waiters of the establishment. This is done by either keeping a tab of the customers' drink orders and then totaling the bill before the customer leaves—the same way the wait staff does for food bills—or by charging for each drink served. In either case, the bartender must be able to calculate the bill quickly and accurately. Although many cash registers automatically total the bill, the bartender must also have a good idea of what customers have ordered to help ensure the cash register receipt is correct.

Bartenders who own their own businesses must also keep their own records, as well as hire, train, and direct their employees.

Today, special machines can automatically mix and dispense certain drinks. They are generally found in larger operations. But even if they became more widespread, they could not replace bartenders.

Bartenders still have the knowledge and expertise needed to fill unusual orders or to dispense drinks manually in case the automatic equipment does not function properly.

In combination taverns and packaged-goods stores, bar attendants also sell unopened bottles of alcoholic and nonalcoholic beverages to be taken from the premises. Taproom attendants prepare and serve glasses or pitchers of draft beer.

One of the more important aspects of a bartender's job is making sure a customer does not drive a car after consuming too much alcohol. The bar and the bartender who sold a customer drinks can be held responsible if the customer is arrested or has an accident while driving under the influence of alcohol. It is no longer just an act of kindness to limit the number of drinks someone has, or to keep someone from driving under the influence; it's the law. The bartender must constantly evaluate the customers being served in the bar. It is the responsibility of the bartender to determine when a customer has had too much alcohol.

Bartenders should also have good listening skills, as the barstool often doubles as an informal confessional. Many people become talkative after a drink or two, and a friendly ear can increase the size of a bartender's tip significantly, and turn a customer into a "regular."

REQUIREMENTS

High School
Because bartenders must be good at calculating tabs, high school math classes are important to take. If you would like to own your own bar someday, consider taking business or accounting classes. You might also take home economics classes to gain exposure to food and beverage measurements and preparation. Communication is a key part of this job. The bartender who can chat with customers, making them feel at home and welcomed, and work well as part of a team will have the most success in this profession. To improve your communication abilities, therefore, take English, speech, and any other classes that offer you the opportunity to work on these skills.

Postsecondary Training
A wide variety of vocational and technical schools offer complete courses in bartending. The American Bartenders Association recommends the completion of formal training to prepare for this work. Such training will not only teach you about mixology (how to make

Bartenders mix drinks by combining exactly the right proportion of liquor, wines, mixers, and other ingredients. (*Getty Images*)

mixed drinks) but also instruct you in areas such as business and marketing. It is important to note, though, that you must be old enough (usually at least 21) to serve alcohol in order to attend bartending school. Many bartenders also learn their trade on the job. They usually have had previous experience as bartender helpers, waiters' assistants, or waiters or waitresses.

Certification or Licensing
Bartenders must be familiar with state and local laws concerning the sale of alcoholic beverages. Although not required to by law, many restaurants and hotels hire bartenders who are certified in alcohol awareness. A bartender and an establishment that serves alcohol can be held liable in accidents or injuries caused by a customer who drinks too much. Most bartending courses include this certification in their training programs and some restaurants and hotels also offer alcohol awareness certification to all employees who serve alcohol.

Other Requirements
Generally, bartenders must be at least 21 years of age, although some employers prefer they be older than 25. Bartenders must be in good physical condition in order to stand comfortably for long periods of time and to lift heavy cases of beverages or kegs of beer. Because they

deal with the public, they must have a pleasant personality and a clean, neat appearance. (Of course, for certain sorts of bars, a clean, neat appearance can be a detriment!) In some states, bartenders must have health certificates assuring that they are free of contagious diseases. Because of the large sums of money collected in some bars, bartenders must sometimes be bonded. Bartenders should also have good common sense, knowing when a customer has had too much to drink, and how to handle uncomfortable social situations. They should also be familiar with a variety of alcoholic beverages—a gin and tonic made with high-quality gin tastes markedly different from one made with ordinary liquor, and the proper technique for pouring a pint of heavy stout from a tap is an art form in itself.

EXPLORING

Because of the age requirement, students under the age of 21 will find it difficult to get actual bartending experience. Part-time or summer jobs as waiters' assistants or waiters, however, will allow you to watch a bartender at work and in that way learn how to mix drinks and perform other bartending tasks. Preparing drinks at home is good experience, although in itself it does not qualify you to become a bartender. Any part-time or summer job that involves serving food and beverages to the public will give you the opportunity to see if you have the right temperament for this occupation.

Further career exploration may include talking with school counselors, visiting vocational schools that offer bartending courses, interviewing bartenders, and reading bar guides and manuals.

EMPLOYERS

Bartenders may be employed in restaurants, bars, hotels, vacation resorts, social clubs, food service establishments, and anywhere alcohol is served to the public. Additionally, they can find work serving alcoholic drinks at private parties and residences. Catering services often hire bartenders to serve at special functions. Fewer than 10 percent are self-employed.

STARTING OUT

Those interested in becoming bartenders often begin by working as bartender helpers, waiters' assistants, or waiters. Small restaurants, neighborhood bars, and vacation resorts usually offer a beginner the best opportunity. Many people tend bar part time while working at other jobs or attending college, often serving at banquets and private parties at restaurants, at hotels, or in private homes. Vocational schools offering bartending courses sometimes help their graduates find jobs.

Application may be made directly to hotels, restaurants, cocktail lounges, and other businesses that serve alcoholic beverages. Some employment agencies specialize in placing hotel and restaurant personnel. Information about job opportunities may also be obtained from the local offices of the state employment service. The Hotel Employees and Restaurant Employees International Union also offers information on bartender apprenticeship programs.

ADVANCEMENT

With experience, a bartender may find employment in a large restaurant or cocktail lounge where the pay is higher. Opportunities for advancement in this field, however, are limited. A few persons may earn promotions to head bartender, wine steward, or beverage manager. Some bartenders go on to open their own taverns or restaurants.

EARNINGS

Earnings for this occupation cover a broad range and are influenced by such factors as the bartender's experience, his or her ability to deal with the public, and even where he or she works. The U.S. Department of Labor reports that full-time bartenders had median hourly wages of $7.42 in 2004. A person working 40 hours a week at this pay rate would earn approximately $15,433 annually. The lowest paid 10 percent of full-time bartenders earned less than $5.72 per hour (or, less than approximately $11,900 annually), and the highest paid 10 percent made more than $12.47 per hour (more than approximately $26,000 annually). These earning figures do not include tips. With tips, bartenders' yearly incomes may increase by thousands of dollars, depending on factors such as the bartender's personality and service he or she gives, the establishment's location, and the size of the bar.

Besides wages and tips, bartenders may get free meals at work and may be furnished bar jackets or complete uniforms. Those who work fulltime usually receive typical benefits, such as health insurance and vacation days.

WORK ENVIRONMENT

Many bartenders work more than 40 hours a week. They work nights, weekends, and holidays, and split shifts are common. They have to work quickly and under pressure during busy periods. Also, they need more strength than average to lift heavy cases of liquor and mixers.

Many bartenders feel the difficulties of the job are more than offset by the opportunity to talk to friendly customers, by the possibility of one day managing or owning a bar or restaurant, or by the need for good part-time work.

It is important that individuals entering this field like people, since they will be in constant contact with the public. Even when the work is hardest and the most hectic, bartenders are expected to be friendly and attentive to their customers. Patrons of a bar will often use the bartender as a sounding board or a confessor. All they really want is a sympathetic ear. Good bartenders will appear interested without getting personally involved in other people's problems.

The success of a restaurant or cocktail lounge depends on satisfied customers. For this reason, teamwork among the serving staff is crucial. Often working in cramped quarters, bartenders must cooperate quickly and willingly with other food and beverage service workers and make their workplace friendly and inviting to customers.

OUTLOOK

Employment for bartenders who is expected to grow more slowly than the average through 2012, according to the U.S. Department of Labor, as casual restaurants, which do not employ bartenders, become even more popular. Because of high turnover in this profession, however, bartending jobs should be readily available. This high turnover rate is due to the fact that many people work as bartenders for a short time as they pursue other careers, or while they are finishing school. Others view a bartending position as the first step on a career ladder that leads them to a career in restaurant or bar management.

FOR MORE INFORMATION

This organization focuses on issues affecting those in hotel and restaurant management, foodservice management, and culinary arts. Among its publications are A Guide to College Programs in Hospitality and Tourism *and* Hosteur, *a Webzine for high school and college students. For information about the broad field of hospitality, contact*

International Council on Hotel, Restaurant & Institutional Education
2810 North Parham, Suite 230
Richmond, VA 23294-4442

Tel: 804-346-4801
http://chrie.org

This organization offers a training program in responsible alcoholic beverage service. For more information, contact
National Restaurant Association Educational Foundation
175 West Jackson Boulevard, Suite 1500
Chicago, IL 60604-2702
Tel: 800-765-2122
Email: info@nraef.org
http://www.nraef.org

Bed and Breakfast Owners

OVERVIEW

A bed and breakfast is an inn, or small hotel, of about four to 20 rooms. *Bed and breakfast owners* either single-handedly, or with the help of spouse and family, provide guests with a comfortable, home-like environment. These workers, sometimes called *innkeepers* or abbreviated to *B & B owners,* clean rooms, assign rooms to guests, keep books and records, and provide some meals. They also actively interact with guests and provide information about tours, museums, restaurants, theaters, and recreational areas. According to a study conducted in 2000 by Professional Association of Innkeepers International (PAII), there are approximately 19,000 bed and breakfasts in the United States. Though a bed and breakfast may be located in the very heart of a large city, most are located in small towns, the country, and along oceans, lakes, or rivers.

HISTORY

Though initially considered nothing more than a bed for weary travelers, inns became, over the centuries, clean and comfortable establishments that provided good rest and good food and served as important community centers. Some of the first Elizabethan theaters were simply the courtyards of English lodges. The lodging houses of the first American colonies were styled after these English inns and were considered so necessary that a law in 18th-century Massachusetts required that towns provide roadside lodging.

QUICK FACTS

School Subjects
Business
Family and consumer science

Personal Skills
Communication/ideas
Leadership/management

Work Environment
Primarily one location
Indoors and outdoors

Minimum Education Level
High school diploma

Salary Range
$7,000 to $75,000 to
  $168,000

Certification or Licensing
Required by certain states

Outlook
About as fast as the average

DOT
N/A

GOE
N/A

NOC
0632

O*NET-SOC
N/A

These early examples of bed and breakfasts thrived for years, until the development of the railroad. Large luxury hotels popped up next to railroad stations and did a booming business. Some inns survived, but many became more like hotels in the process, adding rooms and giving less personal service. Other inns became boarding houses, renting rooms by the week and the month. When people took to the highways in automobiles, lodging changed once again, inspiring the development of motels and tourist camps. It has only been in the last 20 years or so that inns have become popular forms of lodging again, with bed and breakfasts opening up in historic houses and towns. In 1980, there were approximately 5,000 inns in the country; today, that number has almost quadrupled.

THE JOB

Have you ever wanted to vacation with the FBI's Public Enemy #1? Probably not. But in Tucson, Arizona, you can sit in the Jacuzzi of the Dillinger House Bed and Breakfast and imagine yourself the pampered 1930s-era bank robber John Dillinger. Mark Muchmore now owns the house and grounds where Dillinger was captured. Though a house with such history may not seem a natural source for a bed and breakfast, the history actually gives the place a unique distinction in the area. Dillinger's respite in the desert town is part of local legend, and his capture is still celebrated with annual parties and dramatic re-creations in some of Tucson's bars. One of the great appeals of bed and breakfasts are the stories behind them. Though not every bed and breakfast has a history as colorful as that of the Dillinger House, many do have well-documented backgrounds. Bed and breakfast owners therefore become great sources of local history and valuable guides to area sites.

Most of the bed and breakfasts across the country are housed in historical structures: the Victorian houses of Cape May, New Jersey; Brooklyn brownstones; a house in Illinois designed by Frank Lloyd Wright. And many are furnished with antiques. Muchmore owned his house for some time before turning it into a bed and breakfast. A job change inspired him to start a new business, opening up his home to guests. "I had always wanted to do something like this," he says. "I already had the property, a large house, and two adjacent guest houses, so it seemed perfect."

As the name *bed and breakfast* suggests, a good homemade breakfast is an essential part of any inn stay. Muchmore's day starts much earlier than Dillinger's ever did and is likely much more serene; he's typically up at 5:00 A.M. grinding coffee beans, harvesting herbs, and preparing to bake. "I accommodate any and all dietary restrictions," Muchmore says, "and do it in such a way that my guests feel really paid attention to and respected." After serving his guests their breakfast and cleaning up, Muchmore sees to business concerns such as answering email messages, calling prospective guests, and taking reservations. Once the guests have left their rooms, Muchmore can clean the rooms and do some laundry. After grocery shopping, he returns to his office for book work and to prepare brochures for the mail.

Among all the daily tasks, Muchmore reserves time to get to know his guests and to make sure they're enjoying their stay. "I like interacting with my guests," he says. "I like hearing about their jobs, their lives, their likes and dislikes. I love to be able to give them sightseeing suggestions, restaurant tips, and from time to time, little extras like a bowl of fresh citrus from my trees." It is such close attention to detail that makes a bed and breakfast successful. The guests of bed and breakfasts are looking for more personal attention and warmer hospitality than they'd receive from a large hotel chain.

Though the owners of bed and breakfasts are giving up much of their privacy by allowing guests to stay in the rooms of their own homes, they do have their houses to themselves from time to time. Some bed and breakfasts are only open during peak tourist season, and some are only open on weekends. And even those open year-round may often be without guests. For some owners, inconsistency in the business is not a problem; many bed and breakfasts are owned by couples and serve as a second income. While one person works at another job, the other tends to the needs of the bed and breakfast.

The PAII classifies the different kinds of bed and breakfasts. A host home is considered a very small business with only a few rooms for rent. Because of its small size, the owner of a host home may not be required by law to license the business or to have government inspections. Without advertising or signs, these homes are referred to guests primarily through reservation service organizations. A bed and breakfast and bed and breakfast inn are classified as having four to 20 rooms. They adhere to license, inspection, and zoning requirements and promote their businesses through brochures, print ads, and signs. A country inn is considered a bit larger, with six to 30 rooms, and it may serve one meal in addition to breakfast.

REQUIREMENTS

High School

Because you'll essentially be maintaining a home as a bed and breakfast owner, you should take home economics courses. These courses can prepare you for the requirements of shopping and cooking for a group of people, as well as budgeting household finances. But a bed and breakfast is also a business, so you need to further develop those budgeting skills in a business fundamentals class, accounting, and math. A shop class, or some other hands-on workshop, can be very valuable to you; take a class that will teach you about electrical wiring, woodworking, and other elements of home repair.

Postsecondary Training

As a bed and breakfast owner, you're in business for yourself, so there are no educational requirements for success. Also, no one specific degree program will better prepare you than any other. A degree in history or art may be as valuable as a degree in business management. Before taking over a bed and breakfast, though, you may consider enrolling in a hotel management or small business program at your local community college. Such programs can educate you in the practical aspects of running a bed and breakfast, from finances and loans to health and licensing regulations.

Opportunities for part-time jobs and internships with a bed and breakfast are few and far between. Bed and breakfast owners can usually use extra help during busy seasons, but can't always afford to hire a staff. But some do enough business that they can hire a housekeeper or a secretary, or they may have an extra room to provide for an apprentice willing to help with the business.

Certification or Licensing

Though bed and breakfast owners aren't generally certified or licensed as individuals, they do license their businesses, and seek accreditation for their inns from professional organizations such as PAII and the American Bed and Breakfast Association. With accreditation, the business can receive referrals from the associations and can be included in their directories. A house with only a room or two for rent may not be subject to any licensing requirements, but most bed and breakfasts are state regulated. A bed and breakfast owner must follow zoning regulations, maintain a small business license, pass health inspections, and carry sufficient liability insurance.

Other Requirements

Bed and breakfast ownership calls upon diverse skills. You must have a head for business, but you have to be comfortable working among people, outside of an office. You must be creative in the way you maintain the house, paying attention to decor and gardening, but you should also have practical skills in plumbing and other household repair (or you should at least be capable of diagnosing any need for repair). A knowledge of the electrical wiring of your house and the phone lines is valuable. You'll also need an ability to cook well for groups both large and small.

"I'm easygoing," Mark Muchmore says in regard to how he makes his business a success, "and I know how to set, and follow through on, personal and professional goals. I'm also a natural organizer, and pay attention to details." Muchmore also enjoys meeting new people, which is very important. You'll be expected to be a gracious host to all your guests. But you'll also have to maintain rules and regulations; guests of bed and breakfasts expect a quiet environment, and smoking and drinking is often prohibited.

If turning your home into a bed and breakfast, you should learn about city planning and zoning restrictions, as well as inspection programs. Computer skills will help you to better organize reservations, registration histories, and tax records. You should have some knowledge of marketing in order to promote your business by ads, brochures, and on the Internet.

EXPLORING

PAII provides students with a free informational packet about innkeeping, and also puts together an "Aspiring Innkeepers Package" for those interested in the requirements of running a bed and breakfast. PAII publishes a newsletter and books on innkeeping, holds conferences, and maintains a very informative website (http://www. paii.org). If there are inns in your town, interview the owners and spend a day or two with them as they perform their daily duties. The owner may even have part-time positions open for someone to assist with preparing breakfast or cleaning the rooms—employment of staff has increased in the last few years. Some bed and breakfast owners occasionally hire reliable "innsitters" to manage their inns when they're out of town.

Even a job as a motel housekeeper or desk clerk can give you experience with the responsibilities of innkeeping. Bed and breakfasts, hotels, and resorts across the country often advertise nationally for seasonal assistance. For years, high school and college students have made a little extra money working in exotic locales by dedicating their summers to full-time hotel or resort jobs. Wait staff, poolside assistants, kitchen staff, housekeepers, and spa assistants are needed in abundance during peak tourist seasons. In some cases, you can get a paid position, and in others you may be expected to work in exchange for room and board. Even if your summer job is at a large resort rather than a small bed and breakfast, you can still develop valuable people skills and learn a lot about the travel and tourism industry.

EMPLOYERS

Innkeepers work for themselves. The charm of bed and breakfasts is that they are owned and operated by individuals, or individual families, who live on the premises. Though bed and breakfast "chains" may be a thing of the future, they are not expected to greatly affect the business of the traditional "mom and pop" operations.

Most bed and breakfasts exist in rural areas and small towns where there are no large hotels. Though the number of inns in cities is increasing, only 19 percent of the inns in the United States are located in urban areas. According to PAII, the majority of inns (49 percent) are in small resort villages. Thirty-two percent of the inns are in rural areas.

An innkeeper's income is derived from room rental and fees for any "extras" such as additional meals and transportation. An inn's guests are often from outside of the local area, but an inn may also cater to many area residents. Most guests are screened by reservation service organizations or travel associations; this helps to protect both the guest and the owner. Bed and breakfasts must pass certain approval requirements, and guests must prove to be reliable, paying customers.

STARTING OUT

Probably all the bed and breakfast owners you speak to will have different stories about how they came to own their businesses. Some, like Mark Muchmore, convert their own homes into inns; others buy fully established businesses, complete with client lists, marketing plans, and furnishings. Others inherit their bed and breakfasts from family members. And still others lease a house from another owner. Usually, bed and breakfast ownership requires a large investment, both in time and money. Before starting your business, you must do a great deal of research. Make sure the local market can support an additional bed and breakfast and that your house and grounds will offer a unique and attractive alternative to the other lodging in the area. Research how much you can expect to make the first few years, and how much you can afford to lose. Muchmore suggests that you be sure to promote your business, but don't go overboard. "All advertising is not worth it," he says. "I have found that small ads in local publications, one listing in a nationally distributed magazine, a home or Web page, and word of mouth are more than enough."

Established bed and breakfasts for sale are advertised nationally, and by innkeeper associations. Prices range from under $100,000 to over $1,000,000. An established business is often completely restored and includes antique furniture and fixtures, as well as necessary equipment.

ADVANCEMENT

Mark Muchmore sees expansion in the future of the Dillinger House Bed and Breakfast. "I see buying another property in the neighborhood," he says, "and at that point operating as an inn/spa. This would enable me to hire a small staff and include some of the extras for my guests to make them feel even more pampered." With the free time that a staff would provide, Muchmore could dedicate more time to marketing and promotion.

In many cases, a married bed and breakfast owner may continue to work full time outside of the home, while his or her spouse sees to the daily concerns of the inn. But once a business is well-established with a steady clientele, both spouses may be able to commit full-time to the bed and breakfast.

EARNINGS

Large, well-established bed and breakfasts can bring in tens of thousands of dollars every year, but most owners of average-sized inns must make do with much less. A survey by PAII provides a variety of income figures. A beginning bed and breakfast has an annual net operating income of $25,000, while one seven years or older has an average income of over $73,000. A small bed and breakfast with four rooms or fewer for rent has an annual net income of about $7,000; an inn of five to eight rooms has an income of $35,000; nine to 12 rooms, $80,000. An inn with 13 to 20 rooms has a net operating income of over $168,000. Fifty-five percent of bed and breakfast owners are dependent on outside income.

Bed and breakfasts in the western part of the United States make more money than those in other parts of the country. An average net income of $68,000 per year is figured for inns in the West, followed by $58,000 for those in the Northeast, $38,000 in the Southeast, and $33,000 in the Midwest. According to PAII, bed and breakfasts charge from $38 to $595 per day, depending on size of the room and whether it has a private bath, fireplace, and other amenities.

WORK ENVIRONMENT

Imagine yourself living in a beautiful, restored historical house among antiques and vacationers from all around the world. And you don't have to leave to go to work. Though it sounds like an ideal environment, and it may not seem like you're at work, bed and breakfast owners must perform many responsibilities to keep their property nice and pleasant. Their chores will mostly be domestic ones, keeping them close to the house with cooking, cleaning, gardening, and laundering. This makes for a very comfortable work environment over which they have a great deal of control. Though bed and breakfast owners work in their own home, they must sacrifice much of their privacy to operate their business. They must be available to their guests at all times to ensure that their stay is comfortable. However, even the most successful bed and breakfast isn't always full to capacity, and many are only open on weekends—this may result in a few long work days, then a few days of downtime. But to keep their business afloat, bed and breakfast owners will need to welcome as many guests as they can handle.

OUTLOOK

Some bed and breakfasts have been in business for decades, but it's only been in the last 20 years that inns have become popular vacation spots. PAII estimates the number of inns in the country to be approximately 19,000, up from a measly 5,000 in 1980. Tourists are seeking out inns as inexpensive and charming alternatives to the rising cost and sterile, cookie-cutter design of hotels and motels. People are even centering their vacation plans on bed and breakfasts, booking trips to historical towns for restful departures from cities. As long as bed and breakfasts can keep their rates lower than hotel chains, they are likely to flourish.

Recognizing the appeal of bed and breakfasts, some hotel chains are considering plans to capitalize on the trend with "inn-style" lodging. An inn-style hotel is even on its way to Disneyland! Smaller hotels composed of larger, suite-style rooms with more personalized service may threaten the business of some bed and breakfasts. But the charm and historic significance of an old house can't easily be reproduced, so bed and breakfasts are expected to maintain their niche in the tourism industry.

The Americans with Disabilities Act (ADA) will also have some effect on the future of bed and breakfasts. Inns with more than six rooms are required to comply with the ADA, making their rooms and grounds handicapped accessible. When purchasing a property for the purpose of a bed and breakfast, buyers must take into consideration the expense and impact of making such additions and changes. Though some businesses may have trouble complying, those that can will open up an area of tourism previously unavailable to people with disabilities.

FOR MORE INFORMATION

To explore the bed and breakfasts of New England, contact
New England Innkeepers Association
PO Box 1089
44 Lafayette Road, Unit 6
North Hampton, NH 03862-1089
Tel: 603-964-6689
Email: info@newenglandinns.com
http://www.newenglandinns.com

Contact PAII to request their free student packet, which inludes information about innkeepers and their guests, seminars and consultants, and average operating expenses and revenues.
Professional Association of Innkeepers International
207 White Horse Pike
Haddon Heights, NJ 08035
Tel: 856-310-1102
Email: membership@paii.org
http://www.paii.org

Cooks and Chefs

OVERVIEW

Cooks and *chefs* are employed in the preparation and cooking of food, usually in large quantities, in hotels, restaurants, cafeterias, and other establishments and institutions. There are roughly 3.1 million cooks, chefs, and other food preparation workers employed in the United States.

HISTORY

The art of cookery is as ancient as the history of humankind. The early Greeks, Egyptians, and Romans valued cooks as highly respected members of society.

France has given the world some of the finest cooks and chefs. Historical records reflect the avid interest the French people have in the art of cookery. Even today, cooks and chefs who are skilled in the art of French cuisine are highly valued and work in some of the world's most luxurious hotels and restaurants.

The hostelries of early America provided food and rest for weary travelers. Although these inns and taverns sometimes employed cooks specially hired from outside the proprietor's family, the food was often marginal in quality. It was not until hotels were built in the large cities that the occupation of cook developed into a profession.

The pleasure of dining out has become big business in the United States. The public has a range of choices—from the simplest, most inexpensive meal to the most expensive and elaborate. Whether a restaurant prides itself on "home cooking" or on exotic foreign cuisine, its cooks and chefs are largely responsible for the reputation it acquires.

QUICK FACTS

School Subjects
Family and consumer science
Mathematics

Personal Skills
Artistic
Following instructions

Work Environment
Primarily indoors
Primarily one location

Minimum Education Level
Apprenticeship

Salary Range
$14,090 to $19,700 to $27,910

Certification or Licensing
Required by certain states

Outlook
About as fast as the average

DOT
313

GOE
11.05.01

NOC
6241, 6242

O*NET-SOC
35-1011.00, 35-2011.00, 35-2012.00, 35-2014.00, 35-2015.00

THE JOB

Cooks and chefs are primarily responsible for the preparation and cooking of foods. Chefs usually supervise the work of cooks; however, the skills required and the job duties performed by each may vary depending upon the size and type of establishment.

Cooks and chefs begin by planning menus in advance. They estimate the amount of food that will be required for a specified period of time, order it from various suppliers, and check it for quantity and quality when it arrives. Following recipes or their own instincts, they measure and mix ingredients for soups, salads, gravies, sauces, casseroles, and desserts. They prepare meats, poultry, fish, vegetables, and other foods for baking, roasting, broiling, and steaming. They use blenders, mixers, grinders, slicers, or tenderizers to prepare the food, and ovens, broilers, grills, roasters, or steam kettles to cook it. During the mixing and cooking, cooks and chefs rely on their judgment and experience to add seasonings; they constantly taste and smell food being cooked and must know when it is cooked properly. To fill orders, they carve meat, arrange food portions on serving plates, and add appropriate gravies, sauces, or garnishes.

Some larger establishments employ specialized cooks, such as banquet cooks, pastry cooks, and broiler cooks. The *garde-manger* designs and prepares buffets, and *pantry cooks* prepare cold dishes for lunch and dinner. Other specialists are raw shellfish preparers and carvers.

In smaller establishments without specialized cooks, kitchen helpers, or prep cooks, the general cooks may have to do some of the preliminary work themselves, such as washing, peeling, cutting, and shredding vegetables and fruits; cutting, trimming, and boning meat; cleaning and preparing poultry, fish, and shellfish; and baking bread, rolls, cakes, and pastries.

Commercial cookery is usually done in large quantities, and many cooks, including school cafeteria cooks and mess cooks, are trained in "quantity cookery" methods. Numerous establishments today are noted for their specialties in foods, and some cooks work exclusively in the preparation and cooking of exotic dishes, very elaborate meals, or some particular creation of their own for which they have become famous. Restaurants that feature national cuisines may employ *international and regional cuisine specialty cooks*.

In the larger commercial kitchens, chefs may be responsible for the work of a number of cooks, each preparing and cooking food in specialized areas. They may, for example, employ expert cooks who specialize in frying, baking, roasting, broiling, or sauce cookery. Cooks are often titled by the kinds of specialized cooking they do,

A hotel pastry chef ices
a layer of a wedding cake.
(Getty Images)

such as fry, vegetable, or pastry. Chefs have the major responsibility for supervising the overall preparation and cooking of the food.

Other duties of chefs may include training cooks on the job, planning menus, pricing food for menus, and purchasing food. Chefs may be responsible for determining the weights of portions to be prepared and served. Among their other duties may be the supervision of the work of all members of the kitchen staff. The kitchen staff assists by washing, cleaning, and preparing foods for cooking; cleaning utensils, dishes, and silverware; and assisting in many ways with the overall order and cleanliness of the kitchen. Most chefs spend part of their time striving to create new recipes that will win the praise of customers and build their reputations as experts. Many, like pastry chefs, focus their attention on particular kinds of food.

Expert chefs who have a number of years of experience behind them may be employed as *executive chefs*. These chefs do little cooking or food preparation—their main responsibilities are management and supervision. Executive chefs interview, hire, and dismiss kitchen personnel, and they are sometimes responsible for the dining room waiters and other employees. These chefs consult with the restaurant manager regarding the profits and losses of the food service and ways to increase business and cut costs. A part of their time is spent inspecting equipment. Executive chefs are in charge of all food services for special functions such as banquets and parties, and they spend many hours coordinating the work for these activities. They may supervise the special chefs and assist them in planning elaborate arrangements and creations in food preparation. Executive chefs may be assisted by workers called *sous chefs*.

Smaller restaurants may employ only one or two cooks and workers to assist them. Cooks and assistants work together to prepare all the food for cooking and to keep the kitchen clean. Because smaller restaurants and public eating places usually offer standard menus with little variation, the cook's job becomes standardized. Such establishments may employ specialty cooks, barbecue cooks, pizza bakers, food order expediters, kitchen food assemblers, or counter supply workers. In some restaurants food is cooked as it is ordered; cooks preparing food in this manner are known as *short-order cooks*.

Regardless of the duties performed, cooks and chefs are largely responsible for the reputation and monetary profit or loss of the eating establishment at which they are employed.

REQUIREMENTS

The occupation of chef or cook has specific training requirements. Many cooks start out as kitchen helpers and acquire their skills on the job, but the trend today is to obtain training through high schools, vocational schools, or community colleges.

The amount of training required varies with the position. It takes only a short time to become an assistant or a fry cook, for example, but it requires years of training and experience to acquire the skills necessary to become an executive chef or cook in a fine restaurant.

High School
Although a high school diploma is not required for beginning positions, it is an asset to job applicants. If you are interested in moving beyond low-level positions such as kitchen helper or fry cook, your high school education should include classes in family and consumer science and health. These courses will teach you about nutrition, food preparation, and food storage. Math classes are also recommended; in this line of work you must be comfortable working with fractions, multiplying, and dividing. Since chefs and head cooks often have management responsibilities, you should also take business courses.

Postsecondary Training

Culinary students spend most of their time learning to prepare food through hands-on practice. At the same time, they learn how to use and care for kitchen equipment. Training programs often include courses in menu planning, determining portion size, controlling food costs, purchasing food supplies in quantity, selecting and storing food, and using leftovers. Students also learn hotel and restaurant sanitation and public health rules for handling food. Courses offered by private vocational schools, professional associations, and university programs often emphasize training in supervisory and management skills.

Professional associations and trade unions sometimes offer apprenticeship programs; one example is the three-year apprenticeship program sponsored by chapters of the American Culinary Federation (ACF) in cooperation with local employers. This program combines classroom work with on-the-job training under the supervision of a qualified chef and is an excellent way to begin your career. For more information, visit the education section of the ACF website at http://www.acfchefs.org. Some large hotels and restaurants have their own training programs for new employees. The armed forces also offer good training and experience.

Certification or Licensing

To protect the public's health, chefs, cooks, and bakers are required by law in most states to possess a health certificate and to be examined periodically. These examinations, usually given by the state board of health, make certain that the individual is free from communicable diseases and skin infections. ACF offers certification at a variety of levels, such as executive chef and sous chef. In addition to educational and experience requirements, candidates must also pass written tests for each certification. Certification from ACF is recommended as a way to enhance your professional standing and advance your career.

Other Requirements

The successful chef or cook has a keen interest in food preparation and cooking and has a desire to experiment in developing new recipes and new food combinations. Cooks and chefs should be able to work as part of a team and to work under pressure during rush hours, in close quarters, and with a certain amount of noise and confusion. These employees need an even temperament and patience to contend with the public daily and to work closely with many other kinds of employees.

Immaculate personal cleanliness and good health are necessities in this trade. Applicants should possess physical stamina and be without serious physical impairments because of the mobility and activity the work requires. These employees spend many working hours standing, walking, and moving about.

Chefs and cooks must possess a keen sense of taste and smell. Hand and finger agility, hand-eye coordination, and a good memory are helpful. An artistic flair and creative talents in working with food are definitely strengths in this trade.

The principal union for cooks and chefs is the Hotel Employees and Restaurant Employees International Union (affiliated with the AFL-CIO).

EXPLORING

You may explore your interest in cooking right at home. Prepare meals for your family, offer to make a special dessert for a friend's birthday, create your own recipes. Any such hands-on experiences will build your skills and help you determine what type of cooking you enjoy the most.

Volunteer opportunities may be available at local kitchens that serve the homeless or others in need. You can also get a paying part-time or summer job at a fast food or other restaurant. Large and institutional kitchens, for example those in nursing homes, may offer positions such as sandwich or salad maker, soda-fountain attendant, or kitchen helper; while doing one of these jobs, you can observe the work of chefs and cooks.

EMPLOYERS

Cooks and chefs are needed by restaurants of all types and sizes; schools, hospitals, and other institutions; hotels, cruise lines, airlines, and other industries; and catering and bakery businesses. Approximately 60 percent work at restaurants, other retail eateries, and drinking establishments. Roughly 20 percent are employed by institutions/cafeterias, such as schools, hospitals, and nursing homes. The rest work at such places as grocery stores, hotels, and catering businesses.

STARTING OUT

Apprenticeship programs are one method of entering the trade. These programs usually offer the beginner sound basic training and a regular salary. Upon completion of the apprenticeship, cooks may be hired full-time in their place of training or assisted in finding employment with another establishment. Cooks are hired as chefs only after they have acquired a number of years of experience. Cooks who have been formally trained through public or private trade or vocational schools or in culinary institutes may be able to take advantage of school placement services.

In many cases, a cook begins as a kitchen helper or cook's helper and, through experience gained in on-the-job training, is able to move into the job of cook. To do this, people sometimes start out in small restaurants, perhaps as short-order cooks, grill cooks, or sandwich or salad makers, and transfer to larger establishments as they gain experience.

School cafeteria workers who want to become cooks may have an opportunity to receive food-services training. Many school districts, with the cooperation of school food-services divisions of the state departments of education, provide on-the-job training and sometimes summer workshops for interested cafeteria employees. Some community colleges, state departments of education, and school associations offer similar programs. Cafeteria workers who have completed these training programs are often selected to fill positions as cooks.

Job opportunities may be located through employment bureaus, trade associations, unions, contacts with friends, newspaper want ads, or local offices of the state employment service. Another method is to apply directly to restaurants or hotels. Small restaurants, school cafeterias, and other eating-places with simple food preparation will provide the greatest number of starting jobs for cooks. Job applicants who have had courses in commercial food preparation will have an advantage in large restaurants and hotels, where hiring standards are often high.

ADVANCEMENT

Advancement depends on the skill, training, experience, originality, and ambition of the individual. It also depends somewhat on the general business climate and employment trends.

Cooks with experience can advance by moving to other places of employment for higher wages or to establishments looking for someone with a specialized skill in preparing a particular kind of food. Cooks who have a number of years of successful job experience may find chef positions open to them; however, in some cases it may take 10 or 15 years to obtain such a position, depending on personal qualifications and other employment factors.

Expert cooks who have obtained supervisory responsibilities as head cooks or chefs may advance to positions as executive chefs or to other types of managerial work. Some go into business for themselves as caterers or restaurant owners; others may become instructors in vocational programs in high schools, colleges, or other academic institutions.

EARNINGS

The salaries earned by chefs and cooks are widely divergent and depend on many factors, such as the size, type, and location of the establishment, and the skill, experience, training, and specialization of the worker. Salaries are usually fairly standard among establishments of the same type. For example, restaurants and diners serving inexpensive meals and a sandwich-type menu generally pay cooks less than establishments with medium-priced or expensive menus. The highest wages are earned at restaurants and hotels known for their elegance.

The U.S. Department of Labor reports the following earnings for cooks and chefs in a variety of positions. In 2004, the median annual salary for head cooks and chefs was $31,380. The highest paid 10 percent of head cooks and chefs earned more than $56,060 per year. The lowest 10 percent of head cooks and chefs earned less than $18,090 per year. Restaurant cooks had median annual earnings of $19,700, with salaries ranging from less than $14,090 to more than $27,910 per year. Cooks working at institutions or cafeterias had median earnings of approximately $19,330 per year, and short-order cooks earned a median annual salary of approximately $17,210 annually. Cooks at fast food restaurants were at the bottom of the pay scale, earning a median of approximately $14,770 per year). When looking at the earnings, however, you should bear in mind that more than 2 out of 5 food preparation workers are employed part time, and so can count on less annual pay than indicated here.

Chefs and cooks sometimes receive their meals free during working hours and are furnished with any necessary job uniforms. Those working full time usually receive standard benefits, such as health insurance and vacation and sick days.

WORK ENVIRONMENT

Working conditions vary with the place of employment. Many kitchens are modern, well lighted, well equipped, and air-conditioned, but some older, smaller eating-places may be only marginally equipped. The work of cooks can be strenuous, with long hours of standing, lifting heavy pots, and working near hot ovens and ranges. Possible hazards include falls, cuts, and burns, although serious injury is uncommon. Even in the most modern kitchens, cooks, chefs, and bakers usually work amid considerable noise from the operation of equipment and machinery.

Experienced cooks may work with little or no supervision, depending on the size of the food service and the place of employment. Less experienced cooks may work under much more direct supervision from expert cooks or chefs.

Chefs and cooks may work a 40- or 48-hour week, depending on the type of food service offered and certain union agreements. Some food establishments are open 24 hours a day, while others may be open from the very early morning until late in the evening. Establishments open long hours may have two or three work shifts, with some chefs and cooks working day schedules while others work evenings.

All food-service workers may have to work overtime hours, depending on the amount of business and rush-hour trade. These employees work many weekends and holidays, although they may have a day off every week or rotate with other employees to have alternate weekends free. Many cooks are required to work early morning or late evening shifts. For example, doughnuts, breads, and muffins for breakfast service must be baked by 6:00 or 7:00 A.M., which requires bakers to begin work at 2:00 or 3:00 A.M. Some people will find it very difficult to adjust to working such late and irregular hours.

OUTLOOK

Overall the employment of chefs and cooks is expected to increase as fast as the average for all occupations through 2014, according to the U.S. Department of Labor. While some areas (such as cooks in fast food) may not see much growth in number of new jobs, turnover rates are high and the need to find replacement cooks and chefs will mean many job opportunities in all areas. The need for cooks and chefs will also grow as the population increases and lifestyles change. As people earn higher incomes and have more leisure time, they dine out more often and take more vacations. In addition, working parents and their families dine out frequently as a convenience.

FOR MORE INFORMATION

For information on careers in baking and cooking, education, and certification, contact the following organizations:

American Culinary Federation Inc.
180 Center Place
St. Augustine, FL 32095
Tel: 800-624-9458
Email: acf@acfchefs.net
http://www.acfchefs.org

American Institute of Baking
1213 Bakers Way
PO Box 3999
Manhattan, KS 66505-3999
Tel: 785-537-4750
Email: info@aibonline.org
http://www.aibonline.org

Culinary Institute of America
1946 Campus Drive
Hyde Park, NY 12538-1499
Tel: 845-452-9600
http://www.ciachef.edu

**Educational Institute of the American Hotel and
   Lodging Association**
800 North Magnolia Avenue, Suite 1800
Orlando, FL 32803
Tel: 800-752-4567
Email: info@ei-ahla.org
http://www.ei-ahla.org

National Restaurant Association Educational Foundation
175 West Jackson Boulevard, Suite 1500
Chicago, IL 60604-2814
Tel: 800-765-2122
http://www.nraef.org

*For information on culinary schools in Canada, industry news, and
a job bank, visit this organization's website.*
Canadian Culinary Federation
707-1281 West Georgia Street
Vancouver, BC V6E 3J7 Canada
Tel: 506-387-4882
http://www.ccfcc.ca

Cruise Ship Workers

OVERVIEW

Cruise ship workers provide services to passengers on cruise ships. Besides assisting in the operation of the ship, they may serve food and drinks, maintain cabins and public areas, lead shipboard activities, and provide entertainment.

HISTORY

Before airplanes, people relied on water transportation as a means of traveling from one continent to another. The earliest ships were made of wood and used sails or oars to propel them through the water. They were replaced, in the early 19th century, with the steamship, which was invented by Robert Fulton. The first steamship's boilers heated seawater into steam; this was very economical, though it was necessary to stop the engines often to remove salt deposits. In the 20th century, ships turned to coal burning engines for power, and later oil burning engines.

North American Royal Mail Steam Packet Company, more commonly known as the Cunard Line, built the first luxury ocean liner, the *Mauretania*, in 1907. It was 790 feet in length and able to carry up to 2,000 passengers. Such vessels had ballrooms, libraries, beauty parlors, and numerous dining rooms. First class passengers had comfortable accommodations that were set apart from other passengers. Those paying the lowest fares, often called steerage, had small, cramped quarters. At this time, no matter what class fare was paid, everyone had a common priority—to travel from one continent to another. The invention of airplanes changed all this drastically. As a result, airlines affected, if not created, the cruise line industry as we know it today.

The Cunard Tradition

The Cunard Line is considered by many as the standard for the cruise line industry. The Cunard Line was founded by Sir Samuel Cunard as the North American Royal Mail Steam Packet Company in 1840. Cunard's fleet of four wooden steam ships was originally contracted by England's Queen Victoria to deliver mail from Great Britain to North America. Cunard fulfilled his delivery contract and saw the potential to provide weekly transatlantic service for passengers as well. The Cunard Line later merged with the White Star Line (owner of the infamous *Titanic*) to create funding necessary to build the *Queen Elizabeth,* or *QE,* the largest passenger ship at the time and considered the epitome of cruise luxury and elegance. This vessel was followed by the *Queen Elizabeth 2,* also known as the *QE2,* and, in 2004, the *Queen Mary 2 (QM2),* which is touted as the largest and most luxurious cruise ship ever built. Here are some important facts on the Cunard time line.

- Cunard was the first company to take passengers on regularly scheduled transatlantic departure on the *Britannia,* 1840.

- The first ship to be lit with electricity was Cunard's *Servia,* 1881.

- The first steam turbine engine was the *Campania,* 1893.

- The first gym and health center located on a ship was aboard the *Franconia,* 1911.

- First shipboard indoor swimming pool was on the *Aquitania,* 1914.

- Largest passenger ship built (until 1996) was the *QE,* 1940.

- Cunard was the first line to offer three different around the world cruises simultaneously in 1996 with the *QE2, Royal Viking,* and *Sagafjord.*

Source: Cunard website, http://www.cunardline.com

It was faster, and more convenient, to travel by air; soon, most transcontinental travel was done by plane. However, people still turned to ocean travel as a vacation alternative. The Cunard Line offers customers water travel from New York to Europe on their ships *Queen Elizabeth 2* and *Queen Mary 2* combined with travel by jet on the return leg of the trip.

By the 1980s all water travel on cruise lines was for leisure, rather than as transportation. This decade marked tremendous growth for the cruise industry. Cruise lines built bigger, more opulent ships, added exotic ports of call, and gave more choices regarding destination and length of travel. Today, there are cruises to fit just about every interest, taste, and budget. Many times, passengers can take advantage of air and cruise fare packages, along with a pre- or post-cruise land excursion.

THE JOB

Many modern cruise ships are similar to floating resorts offering fine accommodations, gourmet dining, and every possible activity and form of entertainment. It takes a staff of hundreds, and sometimes thousands, to ensure the smooth operation of a cruise ship and the comfort of all passengers. All employees, regardless of their rank, are expected to participate in routine lifesaving and safety drills. Crew organization is divided into six different departments (smaller liners may not have as many divisions of organization); the *captain,* or the *master of the ship,* oversees the entire crew.

Deck. This department is responsible for the navigation of the ship and oversees the maintenance of the hull and deck.

Engine. This staff operates and maintains machinery. Together, deck and engine staffs include officers, carpenters, seamen, maintenance workers, electricians, engineers, repairmen, plumbers, and incinerator operators.

Radio. *Videographers* are responsible for the maintenance and operation of the ship's broadcast booth, including radio and news telecasts. *Telephonists* help passengers place phone calls shoreside.

Medical. *Physicians* treat passengers whose maladies range from seasickness to more serious health problems. *Nurses* assist the doctors and provide first aid.

Steward. This department, one of the largest on board, is concerned with the comfort of all passengers. The food staff includes specially trained *chefs* that prepare meals, ranging from gourmet dinners to more casual fare poolside. The *wait staff* serves guests in the formal dining room and provides room service. *Wine stewards* help passengers with wine choices, and are responsible for maintaining proper inventories aboard the ship. *Bartenders* mix and serve drinks at many stations throughout the ship. From simple blocks of ice, *sculptors* create works of art that are used to decorate dining room buffets. The housekeeping staff is composed of *executive housekeepers* and *room attendants* who keep cabins and staterooms orderly, supply towels and sheets, and maintain public areas throughout the ship.

Pursers. This large department is responsible for guest relations and services. The *chief purser,* much like a hotel's general manager, is the head of this department and is the main contact for passengers regarding the ship's policies and procedures. *Assistant pursers,* considered junior officers, assist the chief with various duties, such as providing guest services, ship information, monetary exchange, postage, safety deposit boxes, and other duties usually associated with the front desk department of a hotel. The *cruise director* heads the cruise staff and plans daily activities and entertainment. The *youth staff director* plans activities and games specifically designed for children. Ships with a casino on board employ *casino workers,* including game dealers, cashiers, keno runners, and slot machine attendants. *Sound and lighting technicians* are needed to provide music and stage lighting for the many entertainment venues found on board. Many entertainers are hired to sing, dance, and perform comedy skits and musical revues. *Dance instructors* teach dance classes ranging from ballroom to country. Also, many employees are hired to work in duty-free shops and souvenir stores, beauty parlors, spas, health clubs, and libraries.

REQUIREMENTS

High School
Cruise lines require at least a high school education, or equivalent, for most entry-level jobs. While in high school, you should concentrate on classes such as geography, sociology, and a foreign language. Fluency in Spanish, French, and Portuguese is highly desirable.

Postsecondary Training
Officer-level positions, or jobs with more responsibility, require college degrees and past work experience. Many employees, especially those on the cruise staff, have an entertainment background. Youth staff members usually have a background in education or recreation.

Certification or Licensing
Most entry-level jobs do not require certification. Some technical positions, such as those in the engine room, may require special training. Physicians and nurses must be licensed to practice medi-

cine. Child-care workers should have experience and proper training in child care. Some cruise line employees may belong to the Seafarers' International Union.

Other Requirements
You will need a valid U.S. passport to work in this field. If you hold a passport from another country, you will need to obtain a work visa. Check with your country's embassy for details and requirements.

Besides having the proper education, experience, and credentials, employers look for applicants who have excellent communication skills, are outgoing, hardworking, friendly, and enjoy working with people. It is important to make a positive impression with the passengers, so cruise ship workers should always be properly groomed, neatly dressed, and well behaved at all times. Inappropriate contact with passengers is not tolerated.

STARTING OUT

Applicants without college degrees and little shipboard experience are usually assigned to entry-level positions such as wait staff or housekeeping. If you have experience in retail sales, then you may be given a job at the duty-free shop; hospitality experience may land you a position in the purser's office.

Nancy Corbin, youth staff department manager for Royal Caribbean International, began her career in the cruise ship industry as a youth counselor. Not satisfied with the ship's program for children, or rather, the lack of, Corbin and her coworkers revised the schedule of activities and turned the ship's youth counselors into a new department—the youth staff. Today, the youth staff oversees art and science activities, pool parties, talent shows, and theme nights for children ages three to 17.

ADVANCEMENT

Nancy Corbin is still very much involved with the youth staff, though she no longer works on board. Rather, she is stationed shoreside as the youth staff department manager and acts as a liaison for all youth staffs on the cruise line. Where does she see herself in the future? "I'd be interested in a director-type role," Corbin says, "Maybe work as a cruise director."

What are other career paths in this industry? With cruise experience, a cruise staff member can advance to assistant cruise director, and in turn become cruise director. Assistant pursers can be promoted to chief purser. Even people in entry-level positions can be promoted to jobs with more responsibility and, of course, better pay. Bussers can become assistant waiters and then head waiters. Room stewards can be promoted to housekeeping manager and supervise a team of cleaners or a specific section of the ship.

EXPLORING

Actually going on a cruise is one of the best ways to explore this industry. Most cruise lines offer competitive prices along with a selection of cruises and destinations. Also consider inland cruises as a less expensive option.

In many cities located near water, such as Chicago, there are cruise tours running up and down the city's lakefront and the Chicago River. Some even provide entertainment and dinner shows. Many talented performers hone their skills before "trying out" with the bigger cruise lines.

Some cruise lines will hire college students for some of their entry-level positions. Don't forget to apply early, as these jobs are quickly filled.

If you live near a cruise line office or headquarters, contact press relations or human resources for a tour of the department.

EMPLOYERS

There are approximately 45 cruise lines with offices in the United States; together, they employ thousands of cruise ship workers. Most employees are contracted to work four or more months at a time. Some major employers include Royal Caribbean International, The Cunard Line, Holland America, and Disney Cruise Line.

EARNINGS

Most cruise ship employees are hired on a contractual basis—anywhere from four to six months for housekeeping, wait staff, and the concessionaires. The size of the cruise line and the region it sails may also affect wages. According to Cruise Services International, the general salary range is between $1,000 and $1,700 per month, plus tips, or $12,000 to $20,400 per year. Some employees count on passengers' tips to greatly supplement their income. Restaurant and house staff workers can stand to earn anywhere from $300 to $600 in weekly tips.

Employee benefits include room and all meals while on board. Most cruise lines offer emergency health coverage to their employees, regardless of the length of contract. Full-time employees are also offered health insurance, paid sick and holiday time, stock options, and company discounts.

WORK ENVIRONMENT

Workers in the cruise line industry shouldn't expect to have a lot of free time. Most cruise ship workers work long hours—eight- to 14-hour days, seven days a week are not uncommon. Many employees spend a number of weeks, usually five or more, working at sea, followed by an extended leave ashore.

Being a people person is important in this industry. Cruise ship workers not only are expected to work well with their coworkers, but they have to live with them, too. Accommodations for the crew are especially tight; usually two to four employees are assigned to a room. The crew has dining areas and lounges separate from the passengers, yet total privacy is rare on a cruise ship. Usually, crew members have little access to public areas on their free time. However, when the ship docks at port, crew members on leave are allowed to disembark and go shoreside.

OUTLOOK

The cruise line industry is one of the fastest growing segments of the travel industry. More than 9.5 million people cruised in 2004, according to Cruise Lines International Association (CLIA). Over 42 new cruise ships will be added to the North American Fleet from 2000 to 2004, according to CLIA. Ships are getting bigger and more opulent, and have become travel destinations in themselves. Larger cruise lines pack their ships with every amenity imaginable, including libraries, spas, casinos, and in the case of Royal Caribbean International's newest fleet addition—a skating rink and a rock climbing wall. Cruise lines are able to tap into every interest by offering theme or special-interest cruises to their passengers. The Cunard Line offers fine art and opera themes, as well as classic antique cars; Holland America has many sports theme cruises ranging from the Olympics to the Super Bowl; many ships plan super bingo and mah-jongg marathons. Several cruise ships are experimenting with smoke-free cruising.

With so many mega-ships in operation, qualified cruise ship workers are still in demand. Entry-level positions such as wait staff and housekeeping will be fairly easy to obtain with the proper paperwork and credentials. A college degree and work experience will be necessary for positions with more responsibility. Fluency in French, Spanish, or Portuguese is a plus. A cruise ship will offer workers the opportunity to travel around the world and meet many people of different nationalities and cultures.

Remember, however, that cruise life is not all fun and travel. Cruise ship workers are expected to work long, hard hours, and be away from their home base for weeks at a time. Many people find the schedule exhausting and opt to find employment ashore.

FOR MORE INFORMATION

For industry information and job opportunities, contact the following cruise lines:

Cunard Cruise Line
6100 Blue Lagoon Drive, Suite 400
Miami, FL 33126
Tel: 800-5-CUNARD
http://www.cunardline.com

Delta Queen Steamboat Company
Robin Street Wharf
1380 Port of New Orleans Place
New Orleans, LA 70130-1890
Tel: 800-543-1949
Email: hr@amcvnola.com
http://www.deltaqueen.com

Disney Cruise Line
PO Box 10210
Lake Buena Vista, FL 32830
Tel: 407-566-SHIP
http://www.dcljobs.com

Holland America Line
300 Elliott Avenue West
Seattle, WA 98119
Tel: 206-281-3535
Email: resume@halw.com
http://www.hollandamerica.com/about/employment.do

Royal Caribbean International
1050 Caribbean Way

Miami, FL 33132
Tel: 305-539-6000
http://www.royalcaribbean.com

CLIA is the official trade organization of the cruise industry. For industry information, contact
Cruise Line International Association (CLIA)
500 Fifth Avenue, Suite 1407
New York, NY 10110
Tel: 212-921-0066
Email: info@cruising.org
http://www.cruising.org

For information on the industry, employment opportunities, and answers to commonly asked questions regarding employment at sea, contact
Cruise Services International
601 Dundas Street West
Box 24070
Whitby, Ontario L1N 8X8, Canada
Tel: 905-430-0361
Email: info@cruisedreamjob.com
http://www.cruisedreamjob.com

For information about the Seafarer's International Union, contact
Seafarer's International Union
5201 Auth Way
Camp Springs, MD 20746
Tel: 301-899-0675
http://www.seafarers.org

Cultural Advisers

OVERVIEW

Cultural advisers, also known as *bilingual consultants,* work with businesses and organizations to help them communicate effectively with others who are from different cultural and linguistic backgrounds. Cultural advisers usually have a specialty such as business management, banking, education, or computer technology. They help bridge both language and cultural barriers in our increasingly global business world.

HISTORY

Communication has always been a challenge when cultures come into contact with each other. In the early days of the United States, settlers and explorers relied on interpreters to assist them. One of those famous interpreters, Sacajawea, a member of the Shoshone Indian tribe, was a precursor of the cultural advisers of today. As she helped guide Meriwether Lewis and William Clark across the West to the Pacific Ocean, she acted as interpreter when they encountered Native American tribes. She also helped the explorers adapt to the different cultures and customs.

Today's cultural advisers work with companies or organizations that need to communicate effectively and do business with other cultures. Cultural advisers are becoming even more valuable because it is now relatively quick and easy to travel throughout the world, and as trade barriers are eliminated.

THE JOB

Cultural advisers work to bridge gaps in communication and culture. They usually have a second specialty that is complemented by their bilingual skills. For example, a banking and finance expert who has traveled extensively in Japan and is familiar with Japanese language and customs would have the marketable skills to become a cultural adviser for American companies interested in doing business in Japan.

Cultural advisers work in a wide variety of settings. They may hold full-time staff positions with organizations or they may work as independent consultants providing services to a number of clients. Cultural advisers work in education. They provide translation services and help foreign or immigrant students adjust to a new culture. They also educate teachers and administrators to make them aware of cultural differences, so that programs and classes can be adapted to include everyone. Colleges and universities that have large international student populations often have cultural advisers on staff.

In industry, cultural advisers train workers in safety procedures and worker rights. The health care industry benefits from the use of advisers to communicate with non-English-speaking patients. Cultural advisers also hold training sessions for health care professionals to teach them how to better understand and instruct their patients.

Large business enterprises that have overseas interests hire cultural advisers to research new markets and help with negotiations. Some advisers work primarily in employment, finding foreign experts to work for American businesses or finding overseas jobs for American workers. In addition to advising American business leaders, cultural advisers sometimes work with foreign entities that want to do business in the United States. They provide English language instruction and training in American business practices.

Cultural advisers also work in the legal system, the media, advertising, the travel industry, social services, and government agencies. Whatever the setting, cultural advisers help their clients—foreign and American—understand and respect other cultures and communicate effectively with each other.

REQUIREMENTS

High School

Classes in business, speech, and foreign language will give you an excellent head start to becoming a cultural adviser. In addition, take other classes in your high school's college prep curriculum. These courses should include history, mathematics, sciences, and English. Accounting classes and computer science classes will also help prepare you for working in business.

Postsecondary Training

If you are planning a career as a cultural adviser, fluency in two or more languages is a requirement, so college courses in those languages are necessary. Courses in business, world history, world geography, and sociology would be useful as well. You will need at least a bachelor's degree to find work as a cultural adviser, and you may want to consider pursuing a master's degree to have more job opportunities. Many universities offer programs in cultural studies, and there are master's programs that offer a concentration in international business.

Take advantage of every opportunity to learn about the people and area you want to work with, whether Latin America, Europe, Japan, or another region or country. Studying abroad for a semester or year is also recommended.

Other Requirements

Cultural sensitivity is the number one requirement for an adviser. Knowing the history, culture, and social conventions of a people as well as the language is a very important part of the job. Also, expertise in another area, such as business, education, law, or computers, is necessary to be a cultural adviser.

EXPLORING

A good way to explore this field is to join one of your high school's foreign language clubs. In addition to using the foreign language, these clubs often have activities related to the culture where the language is spoken. You may also find it helpful to join your school's business club, which will give you an opportunity to learn about business tactics and finances, as well as give you an idea of how to run your own business.

Learn as much as you can about people and life in other parts of the world. You can do this by joining groups such as American Field Service International (AFS) and getting to know a student from another country who is attending your school. There are also study-abroad and living-abroad programs you can apply to even while in high school. Rotary International and AFS offer such opportunities; see the end of the article for contact information.

EMPLOYERS

Cultural advisers are employed on a contract- or project-basis by businesses, associations, and educational institutions. Large global companies are the most significant source of employment for cultural advisers as they seek to serve the global population. Small to medium-sized companies that do business in a particular region also employ cultural advisers.

Companies in large cities offer the most opportunities for cultural advisers, especially those cities that border other countries and their economies.

Miguel Orta is a cultural adviser in North Miami Beach, Florida. He works with Latin American companies and American companies doing business in Central America and South America. He also has a background in law and business management. Orta is fluent in English, Spanish, and Portuguese. He uses his location in Florida to help businesses in the United States interact with a growing Hispanic population. His Florida location also allows him to be only a short plane flight from his Latin American clients.

STARTING OUT

Most cultural advisers do not begin this career right after college. Some life experience is necessary to be qualified to fill the cultural adviser's role. "Education is very important," says Miguel Orta. "But first you need some work in the trenches." Once that experience is obtained, you will be ready to try advising.

After graduating with a law degree, Orta spent several years as a private attorney representing many Latin American clients. He practiced corporate, international, and labor law. When the opportunity came to serve one of his Venezuelan clients as a cultural adviser, Orta enjoyed the work and decided to become an adviser to others in need of those services.

ADVANCEMENT

Working with larger companies on more extensive projects is one way for a cultural adviser to advance. If an adviser decides to trade in the flexibility and freedom of the job, opportunities to become a salaried employee would most likely be available.

EARNINGS

Cultural advisers are well compensated for the time they spend on projects. Rates can range from approximately $65 to as high as $265 per hour. The median rate is close to $100 per hour. Cultural advisers tend to work on a project-basis and are therefore not guaranteed full-time employment. Advisers may incur business expenses, but their clients generally pay many of the expenses associated with the work, such as travel, meals, and lodging.

WORK ENVIRONMENT

The work environment of cultural advisers largely depends on their specialties. A smaller company may offer a more informal setting than a multinational corporation. A cultural adviser who is employed by a large, international bank may travel much more than an adviser who works for an educational institution or association.

While cultural advisers generally work independently on projects, they must also communicate with a large number of people to complete their tasks. In the middle of a project, a cultural adviser may work 50 to 60 hours per week and travel may be necessary. Between projects, cultural advisers manage their businesses and solicit new clients.

OUTLOOK

The field of cultural advising is predicted to grow faster than the average in the next decade. Demand will grow as trade barriers are continually loosened and U.S. companies conduct more business on a global scale. Latin America and Asia are two promising areas for American businesses.

Cultural advisers will also be needed to address the interests of the increasingly diverse population of the United States. However, competition is keen, and those with graduate degrees and specific expertise will be the most successful.

FOR MORE INFORMATION

Management consulting firms employ a large number of cultural advisers. For more information on the consulting business, contact
Association of Career Firms International
204 E Street, NE
Washington, DC 20002
Tel: 202-547-6344
Email: aocfi@aocfi.org
http://www.aocfi.org

For information about cultural exchanges, contact the following:
American Field Service International
71 West 23rd Street, 17th Floor
New York, NY 10010

Tel: 212-807-8686
Email: info@afs.org
http://www.afs.org

Rotary International
One Rotary Center
1560 Sherman Avenue
Evanston, IL 60201
Tel: 847-866-3000
http://www.rotary.org

For information on etiquette and cross-cultural training, contact
Multi-Language Consultants, Inc.
Tel: 212-726-2164
Email: contact@mlc.com
http://www.mlc.com

Protocol Advisors Inc.
35 Pinckney Street
Boston, MA 02114
Tel: 617-227-2220
http://www.protocoladvisors.com

Flight Attendants

OVERVIEW

Flight attendants are responsible for the safety and comfort of airline passengers from the initial boarding to disembarkment. They are trained to respond to emergencies and passenger illnesses. Flight attendants are required on almost all national and international commercial flights. There are approximately 102,000 flight attendants employed in the United States.

HISTORY

Although the first commercial passenger flights occurred as early as 1911, early airplane flights were not very comfortable. Airplanes were unstable, relatively small, and could not achieve very high altitudes. It was also difficult to operate passenger service at a profit. In the United States, the commercial aviation industry did not take off until the Kelly Air Mail Act of 1925, which encouraged the growth of the first commercial airlines. For many years, commercial airlines prospered because of profits from their airmail business. The government, in an effort to encourage passenger travel, offered airlines subsidies to lower the price of passenger tickets.

Concerns about the safety of airplanes kept many people from flying. In 1926, however, the Air Commerce Act, which established regulations and requirements for pilots and airlines and also defined an air-traffic system, improved consumer confidence in the airline industry. The famous flight of Charles Lindbergh in the following year did much to promote public excitement about flying. Improvements such as stronger engines, better radio and navigational aids, and weather forecasting techniques were making flights safer. An important advancement in commercial air travel came with the development of the pressurized cabin. This invention meant that passengers could fly unaffected by the thin air of higher altitudes. As more people began to fly, the airlines sought ways to make flights even safer, more comfortable, and more enjoyable for their passengers. United Airlines was the first to offer special service to passengers in flight. In 1930, it hired graduate nurses to tend to passengers' comfort and needs. They were called *stewardesses*, after the similar position on cruise ships. Soon after, other airlines added stewardesses to their flights as well. At first, stewardesses performed many functions for the airlines, often acting as mechanics, refueling airplanes, loading passenger luggage and equipment necessary for the flight, as well as cleaning the interior of the airplane. But as airplanes grew larger and the numbers of passengers increased, these positions were filled by specialized personnel, and the stewardesses' responsibilities were devoted to the passengers. Stewardesses also began preparing and serving meals and drinks during flights.

The increasing growth and regulation of the airline industry brought still more duties for the flight attendant. Flight attendants began to instruct passengers on proper safety procedures, and they were required to make certain that safety factors were met before takeoff.

In the early years, most flight attendants were women, and the airlines often required that they remain unmarried in order to retain their jobs. Airlines also instituted age, height, and weight restrictions. Flight attendants were expected to provide a glamorous and pleasant image for airlines. During this time, employee turnover was very high. However, as the role of the flight attendant became more important and as regulations required them to perform more safety-oriented tasks, the image of the flight attendant changed as well. Because training flight attendants was expensive, the airlines began to offer better benefits and other incentives and removed some of their employee restrictions. Experience was also rewarded with higher pay, better benefits, and seniority privileges given according to the number of years worked. More and more flight attendants were making a career with the airlines. The introduction of Federal Aviation Administration (FAA) regulations requiring at least one flight attendant for every 50 passengers gave even greater growth and job security to this career.

Today, flight attendants fill more positions than any other airline occupation. They play a vital role in maintaining passenger safety and comfort in the skies. Many airlines are easing still more of their restrictions, such as age and weight limitations, as the role of the flight attendant has changed to require special training and skills.

THE JOB

Flight attendants perform a variety of preflight and in-flight duties. At least one hour before takeoff, they attend a briefing session with the rest of the flight crew; carefully check flight supplies, emergency life jackets, oxygen masks, and other passenger safety equipment; and see that the passenger cabins are neat, orderly, and furnished with pillows and blankets. They also check the plane galley to see that food and beverages are on board and that the galley is secure for takeoff.

Attendants welcome the passengers on the flight and check their tickets as they board the plane. They show the passengers where to store briefcases and other small pieces of luggage, direct them to their cabin section for seating, and help them put their coats and carry-on luggage in overhead compartments. They often give special attention to elderly or disabled passengers and those traveling with small children.

Before takeoff, a flight attendant speaks to the passengers as a group, usually over a loudspeaker. He or she welcomes the passengers and gives the names of the crew and flight attendants, as well as weather, altitude, and safety information. As required by federal law, flight attendants demonstrate the use of lifesaving equipment and safety procedures and check to make sure all passenger seatbelts are fastened before takeoff.

Upon takeoff and landing and during any rough weather, flight attendants routinely check to make sure passengers are wearing their safety belts properly and have their seats in an upright position. They may distribute reading materials to passengers and answer any questions regarding flight schedules, weather, or the geographic terrain over which the plane is passing. Sometimes they call attention to points of interest that can be seen from the plane. They observe passengers during the flight to ensure their personal comfort and assist anyone who becomes airsick or nervous.

During some flights, attendants serve prepared breakfasts, lunches, dinners, or between-meal refreshments. They are responsible for certain clerical duties, such as filling out passenger reports and issuing reboarding passes. They keep the passenger cabins neat and comfortable during flights. Attendants serving on international flights may provide customs and airport information and sometimes translate flight information or passenger instructions into a foreign language. Most flight attendants work for commercial airlines. A small number, however, work on private airplanes owned and operated by corporations or private companies.

A flight attendant instructs passengers on how to properly fasten safety belts. *(Getty Images)*

REQUIREMENTS

High School

Flight attendants need to have at least a high school education. A broad education is important to allow flight attendants to cope with the variety of situations they will encounter on the job. Beginning foreign language studies in high school will open up the possibility of working on international flights later.

Postsecondary Training

Applicants with college-level education are often given preference in employment. Business training and experience working with the public are also assets. Attendants employed by international airlines are usually required to be able to converse in a foreign language.

Most large airline companies maintain their own training schools for flight attendants. Training programs may last from four to seven weeks. Some smaller airlines send their applicants to the schools run by the bigger airlines. A few colleges and schools offer flight attendant training, but these graduates may still be required to complete an airline's training program.

Airline training programs usually include classes in company operations and schedules, flight regulations and duties, first aid, grooming, emergency operations and evacuation procedures, flight terminology, and other types of job-related instruction. Flight attendants also receive 12 to 14 hours of additional emergency and passenger procedures training each year. Trainees for international flights are given instruction on customs and visa regulations and are taught procedures for terrorist attacks. Near the end of the training period, trainees are taken on practice flights, in which they perform their duties under supervision.

An on-the-job probationary period, usually six months, follows training school. During this time, experienced attendants pay close attention to the performance, aptitudes, and attitudes of the new attendants. After this period, new attendants serve as reserve personnel and fill in for attendants who are ill or on vacation. While on call, these reserve attendants must be available to work on short notice.

Other Requirements
Airlines in the United States require flight attendants to be U.S. citizens, have permanent resident status, or have valid work visas. In general, applicants must be at least 18 to 21 years old, although some airlines have higher minimum age requirements. They should be at least five feet, two inches tall in order to reach overhead compartments, and their weight should be in proportion to their height.

Airlines are particularly interested in employing people who are intelligent, poised, resourceful, and able to work in a tactful manner with the public. Flight attendants must have excellent health, good vision, and the ability to speak clearly. Young people who are interested in this occupation need to have a congenial temperament, a pleasant personality, and the desire to serve the public. They must be able to think clearly and logically, especially in emergency situations, and they must be able to follow instructions working as team members of flight crews.

EXPLORING
Opportunities for experience in this occupation are almost nonexistent until you have completed flight attendant training school. You may explore this occupation by talking with flight attendants or people in airline personnel offices. Airline companies and private training schools publish many brochures describing the work of flight attendants and send them out upon request.

Any part-time or full-time job in customer service, such as food service, hospitality, or retail sales, would offer a good introduction to the kind of work flight attendants do. You might also try volunteering for jobs that require people skills, such as diplomacy, listening, helping, and explaining.

EMPLOYERS

Approximately 102,000 professionally trained flight attendants are employed in the United States. Commercial airlines employ the vast majority of all flight attendants, most of whom are stationed in the major cities that serve as their airline's home base. A very small number of flight attendants work on company-owned or private planes.

STARTING OUT

Individuals who are interested in becoming flight attendants should apply directly to the personnel divisions of airline companies. The names and locations of these companies may be obtained by writing to the Air Transport Association of America. Addresses of airline personnel division offices can also be obtained from almost any airline office or ticket agency. Some major airlines have personnel recruiting teams that travel throughout the United States interviewing prospective flight attendants. Airline company offices can provide interested people with information regarding these recruitment visits, which are sometimes announced in newspaper advertisements in advance.

ADVANCEMENT

A number of advancement opportunities are open to flight attendants. They may advance to supervisory positions such as *first flight attendant* (sometimes known as the *flight purser* or the *supervising flight attendant*), or become an instructor or airline recruitment representative. They may also have the opportunity to move into the position of *chief attendant,* representing all flight attendants in a particular division or area. Although the rate of turnover in this field was once high, more people are making careers as flight attendants, and competition for available supervisory jobs is very high.

Many flight attendants who no longer qualify for flight duty because of health or other factors move into other jobs with the airlines. These jobs may include reservation agent, ticket agent, or personnel recruiter. They may also work in the public relations, sales, air transportation, dispatch, or communications divisions. Trained flight attendants may also find similar employment in other transportation or hospitality industries such as luxury cruise ship lines.

EARNINGS

Beginning flight attendants earned a median salary of $15,552 a year in 2004, according to the Association of Flight Attendants, although earnings vary by airline. Median annual earnings of all flight attendants were $43,440 in 2004, according to the *Occupational Outlook Handbook*. The middle 50 percent earned between $31,310 and $67,590. Salaries ranged from less than $23,450 for the lowest paid 10 percent to more than $95,850 for the highest paid 10 percent. Wage and work schedule requirements are established by union contract. Most flight attendants are members of the Transport Workers Union of America or the Association of Flight Attendants.

Flight attendants are limited to a specific number of flying hours. In general, they work approximately 80 hours of scheduled flying time and an additional 35 hours of ground duties each month. They receive extra compensation for overtime and night flights. Flight attendants on international flights customarily earn higher salaries than those on domestic flights. Most airlines give periodic salary increases until a maximum pay ceiling is reached. Flight assignments are often based on seniority, with the most senior flight attendants having their choice of flight times and destinations.

Airlines usually pay flight attendants in training either living expenses or a training salary. Companies usually pay flight attendants' expenses such as food, ground transportation, and overnight accommodations while they are on duty or away from home base. Some airlines may require first-year flight attendants to furnish their own uniforms, but most companies supply them.

Fringe benefits include paid sick leave and vacation time, free or reduced air travel rates for attendants and their families, and, in some cases, group hospitalization and life insurance plans and retirement benefits.

WORK ENVIRONMENT

Flight attendants are usually assigned to a home base in a major city or large metropolitan area. These locations include cites such as New York, Chicago, Boston, Atlanta, Miami, Los Angeles, San Francisco, and St. Louis. Some airlines assign attendants on a rotation system to home bases, or they may give preference to the requests of those with rank and seniority on bids for certain home bases. Those with the longest records of service may be given the most desirable flights and schedules.

Flight attendants need to be flexible in their work schedules, mainly because commercial airlines maintain operations 24 hours a day throughout the entire year. They may be scheduled to work nights, weekends, and holidays, and they may find that some of their allotted time off occurs away from home between flights. They are often away from home for several days at a time. They work long days, but over a year's time, a flight attendant averages about 156 days off, compared with 96 days off for the average office worker.

The work performed by flight attendants may be physically demanding in some respects. For most of the flight, they are usually on their feet servicing passengers' needs, checking safety precautions, and, in many cases, serving meals and beverages. Working with the public all day can be draining. Flight attendants are the most visible employees of the airline, and they must be courteous to everyone, even passengers who are annoying or demanding. There is a certain degree of risk involved in any type of flight work. Flight attendants may suffer minor injuries as they perform their duties in a moving aircraft. They may suffer from irregular sleeping and eating patterns, dealing with stressful passengers, working in a pressurized environment, and breathing recycled air. Flight attendants also face risk of injury or death from hijackings. Since September 11, 2001, comprehensive security measures and upgrades have been implemented by airlines and the Department of Transportation to ensure the safety of travelers and industry workers.

The combination of free time and the opportunity to travel are benefits that many flight attendants enjoy. For those who enjoy helping and working with people, being a flight attendant may be a rewarding career.

OUTLOOK

The U.S. Department of Labor predicts that employment opportunities for flight attendants will grow about as fast as the average through 2014. The terrorist attacks of September 11, 2001 had a great impact on the airline industry and several thousand flight attendants were laid off. The airline industry predicts a slow economic recovery as passengers only gradually return to the skies in pre–terrorist attack numbers. Economic and political conditions are likely to affect all airline employees over the next few years.

Even in the best of times, finding employment as a flight attendant is highly competitive. Since some job restrictions at airlines have been abolished, and since this career is being viewed in a more professional light than it once was, the high rate of turnover for flight attendants has declined. Even though the number of job openings is expected to grow, airlines receive thousands of applications each year. Most of the job openings through 2014 will arise from replacement of flight attendants who retire or transfer to other jobs. Students interested in this career will have a competitive advantage if they have at least two years of college and prior work experience in customer relations or public contact. Courses in business, psychology, sociology, geography, speech, communications, first aid and emergency medical techniques such as CPR, and knowledge of foreign languages and cultures will make the prospective flight attendant more attractive to the airlines.

FOR MORE INFORMATION

For industry and statistical information, as well as to read the Airline Handbook *online, visit ATA's website.*
  Air Transport Association (ATA)
  1301 Pennsylvania Avenue, NW, Suite 1100
  Washington, DC 20004-1707
  Tel: 202-626-4000
  Email: ata@airlines.org
  http://www.airlines.org

For information on aviation safety, statistics, and regulations, contact
  Federal Aviation Administration
  800 Independence Avenue, SW, Room 810
  Washington, DC 20591
  http://www.faa.gov

This website offers information on careers and job issues and links to discussion forums and other aviation-related sites.
  Flight Attendants.org
  http://www.flightattendants.org

Food Service Workers

OVERVIEW

Food service workers include waiters, counter attendants, dining room attendants, hosts, fast food workers, kitchen assistants, and others. These workers take customers' orders, serve food and beverages, make out customers' checks, and sometimes take payments. These basic duties, however, may vary greatly depending on the specific kind of food service establishment. There are approximately 6.8 million people working as waiters, helpers, attendants, hosts, and other food servers in the United States.

HISTORY

While food service workers make up a large and respected occupational group, it is only in relatively recent times that serving customers in public eating places has become recognized as a separate occupation. In ancient and medieval times, inns were established along main highways to provide food and lodging for travelers. Usually, the innkeeper and his or her family, with perhaps a few servants, were able to look after all the needs of travelers. Restaurants as we know them today hardly existed. Wealthy people did almost all their entertaining in their own homes, where they had large staffs of servants to wait on their guests.

Improved roads and transportation methods in the 18th and 19th centuries led to an increase in travel for both business and pleasure. Inns near large cities, no longer merely havens for weary travelers, became pleasant destinations for day excursions into the country. The rise of an urban middle class created a demand for restaurants where people could enjoy good food and socialize in a convivial

School Subjects
Family and consumer science
Mathematics

Personal Skills
Following instructions
Helping/teaching

Work Environment
Primarily indoors
Primarily one location

Minimum Education Level
High school diploma

Salary Range
$4,430 to $14,040 to
$23,441 plus tips

Certification or Licensing
Required by all states

Outlook
About as fast as the average

DOT
311

GOE
11.05.02

NOC
6641

O*NET
35-2021.00, 35-3022.00,
35-3031.00, 35-9011.00

atmosphere. More and more waiters were needed to serve the growing number of customers. In the great hotels and restaurants of Europe in the 19th century, the presentation of elegantly prepared food in a polished and gracious manner was raised to a high art.

In the United States, the increasing ease and speed of travel has contributed to a very mobile population, which has created a greater demand for commercial food service. People eat at restaurants and fast food establishments more and more. Today, the food service industry is among the largest and most active sectors of the nation's economy.

THE JOB

Food service workers have a variety of job duties depending on the size and kind of food establishment in which they are employed. In small restaurants, sandwich shops, grills, diners, fast food outlets, and cafeterias, customers are usually looking for hot food and quick service. Informal waiters, servers, and lunchroom or coffee shop counter attendants work to satisfy patrons and give them the kind of attention that will make them repeat customers. They take customers' orders, serve food and beverages, calculate bills, and sometimes collect money. Between serving customers, waiters in small establishments may clear and clean tables and counters, replenish supplies, and set up table service for future customers. When business is slow, they spend some time cleaning the serving area and equipment such as coffee machines and blenders. *Combined food preparation and serving workers* work specifically at fast food establishments. They are the people who take food and drink orders from customers at the counter or drive-through window. They also bring the ordered items to the customers and take payment. During quiet periods at the restaurant, they may be responsible for such chores as making coffee, cooking french fries, or cleaning tables. *Counter attendants* in lunchrooms, coffee shops, and diners often do some simple cooking tasks, such as making sandwiches, salads, and cold drinks and preparing ice cream dishes. They also may have to help with such tasks as cleaning kitchen equipment, sweeping and mopping floors, and carrying out trash. Other workers in this category include cafeteria counter attendants, supervisors, canteen operators, and fountain servers.

In larger and more formal restaurants, *waiters,* or *servers,* perform essentially the same services as those working in smaller establishments, but they usually have extra duties designed to make the dining experience more enjoyable. These duties may include seating the customers, presenting them with menus, suggesting choices from the menu, informing the customers of special preparations and seasonings of food, and sometimes suggesting beverages that would complement the meal. They check to see that the correct dinnerware and utensils are on the table and try to attend to any special requests the customers may have.

Servers in expensive restaurants serve food following more formal and correct procedures. *Captains, headwaiters, maitre d's,* and *hosts or hostesses* may greet and seat the guests, take reservations over the phone, and supervise the service of the waiters. *Wine stewards* assist customers in selecting wines from the restaurant's available stock.

Dining room attendants, also known as *waiters' assistants, buspersons,* or *bussers,* assist the waiters in their duties. They may clear and reset tables, carry soiled dishes to the dishwashing area, carry in trays of food, and clean up spilled food and broken dishes. In some restaurants, these attendants also serve water and bread and butter to customers. During slow periods, they may fill salt and pepper shakers, clean coffeepots, and do various other tasks. *Cafeteria attendants* clear and set tables, carry trays of dirty dishes to the kitchen, check supplies, and sometimes serve coffee to customers.

While dining room and cafeteria attendants assure clean and attractive table settings in the dining areas, *kitchen assistants* help maintain

A waiter at a hotel café presents a party with their check. (*Getty Images*)

an efficient and hygienic kitchen area by cleaning food preparation and storage areas, sweeping and scrubbing floors, and removing garbage. They may also move supplies and equipment from storage to work areas, perform some simple food preparation, and wash the pots and pans used in cooking. To keep the kitchen operating smoothly, they maintain a steady supply of clean dishes by scraping food from plates, stacking dishes in and removing them from the dishwasher, polishing flatware, and removing water spots from glasses.

Some food servers may be designated by the place in which they work or the type of specialized service they perform, such as carhops and dining car, room service, takeout, buffet, and club waiters.

REQUIREMENTS

High School

Applicants for jobs as waiters or other food service workers usually do not need a high school diploma. Most employers, however, favor applicants with some high school training, and graduation from high school is generally considered a personal asset, especially if you are planning a career in this industry. While in high school, take family and consumer science classes to learn about food preparation, storage, and presentation. Take basic math classes because you will frequently be dealing with money and will need to do addition, subtraction, and division. At some restaurants waiters carry a certain amount of money with them and make change for customers' bills right at the tables. To do this, you must make quick and accurate calculations in your head. English and speech classes should help you develop your communications skills, which are very important for waiters to have. If you have hopes of moving into management positions or owning your own food business someday, take business and accounting classes as well.

Postsecondary Training

Vocational schools may offer special training courses for waiters. Special courses are sometimes offered by restaurant associations in conjunction with schools or food agencies, and many employers seek persons who have had such training.

Smaller, more informal restaurants may hire servers who are without special training or previous experience. In these situations, the necessary skills are learned on the job. Larger restaurants and those with more formal dining atmospheres usually hire only experienced waiters. Almost without exception, food counter workers, waiters' assistants, and kitchen helpers learn their skills on the job.

Certification or Licensing

Food service workers almost always are required to obtain health certificates from the state Department of Public Health that certify they are free from communicable diseases, as shown by physical examination and blood tests. This is required for the protection of the general public.

The principal union for waiters, food counter workers, waiters' assistants, and kitchen helpers is the Hotel Employees and Restaurant Employees International Union (AFL-CIO); however, not all employees are union members.

Other Requirements

Food service workers generally must be free from any physical disabilities that would impair their movements on the job. They must possess strong physical stamina, because the work requires many long hours of standing and walking. Waiters and food counter workers need to have a congenial temperament, patience, and the desire to please and be of service to the public. All food service workers must be neat and clean in their personal hygiene and dress. Those who serve the public should present a pleasant appearance, be able to communicate well, and be able to use basic arithmetic skills to compute customers' checks. In some restaurants that specialize in the foods of a certain country, servers might need to speak a foreign language. A good memory and persuasive skills are additional personal assets for this occupation.

EXPLORING

Explore this work by getting part-time or summer work as a dining room attendant, counter worker, or waiter at a restaurant, grill, or coffee shop with a casual atmosphere. Volunteer opportunities that combine some type of food service and interaction with the public may also be available in your area. Meals on Wheels, shelters serving meals, and catering services are all sources to consult for volunteering opportunities.

Dealing with the public is a large aspect of food service work, so get experience in this area. If you are unable to find a food service position, get a part-time or summer job as a store clerk, cashier, or other worker directly involved with the public.

EMPLOYERS

The food service industry is one of the largest and most active sectors of the nation's economy. Employers include small restaurants (such as grills, sandwich shops, tearooms, soda shops, and diners), larger restaurants, hotel dining rooms, ships, trains; hospitals, schools, factories; and many other establishments where food is served.

STARTING OUT

People usually enter this field by applying in person for open positions. Job openings are frequently listed in newspaper advertisements, or they may be located through local offices of the state employment service or private employment agencies. The private agencies may charge a percentage fee for their placement services. In some areas where food service workers are unionized, potential employees may seek job placement assistance by contacting union offices.

ADVANCEMENT

Employees may advance to better-paying jobs by transferring to larger and more formal restaurants. They also may gain better positions and higher pay as they obtain more training and experience.

In general, advancement in this field is limited. Nevertheless, waiters may earn promotions to positions as headwaiters, hosts or hostesses, captains, or other supervisors. A waiter may be promoted eventually to restaurant manager, depending on training, experience, and work performance record, as well as on the size and type of food establishment. Food counter workers can advance to cashiers, cooks, waiters, counter or fountain supervisors, or line supervisors in cafeterias. Large organizations, such as fast food or other restaurant chains, may have management training programs or less formal on-the-job training for dependable workers who have leadership ability. Promotion opportunities are much more limited for waiters' assistants and kitchen helpers. Some of them become waiters, cooks' assistants, or short-order cooks; these promotions are more likely to happen in large restaurants and institutions. Some of these higher positions require reading, writing, and arithmetic skills, which employees seeking promotion should keep in mind.

Advancement usually involves greater responsibilities and higher pay. In some cases, a promotion may mean that the employee has the chance to earn more in service tips than in actual salary increases, depending on the size, type, and location of the establishment.

Some individuals may aspire to owning their own businesses or to entering into business partnerships after they have earned and reserved some capital and gained the necessary training and experience. Knowledge of the restaurant and food service business from the inside can be a definite advantage to someone opening or buying a restaurant.

EARNINGS

The earnings of food service workers are determined by a number of factors, such as the type, size, and location of the food establishment, union membership, experience and training of the workers, basic wages paid, and, in some cases, tips earned. Estimating the average wage scale is therefore difficult and has a wide margin of error. It should also be noted that two out of five food service workers, and half of waiters, worked part time, so the annual wages mentioned here would not be applicable for below full-time work.

Waiters depend a great deal on tips to supplement their basic wages, which in general are relatively small. According to the U.S. Department of Labor, waiters earned a median hourly wage of $6.75 (including tips) in 2004. At this pay rate, a person working a 40-hour workweek on a full-time basis would earn approximately $14,040 annually. The department also reports that the highest paid 10 percent of waiters earned more than $11.27 per hour (approximately $23,441 annually), and the lowest paid 10 percent made less than $5.60 per hour ($11,648) in 2004. Tips, usually ranging from 15 to 20 percent of the customers' checks, often amount to more than the actual wages, especially in the larger metropolitan areas. Naturally, waiters working in busy, expensive restaurants earned the most.

The department also reports the following figures for full-time workers in various positions. (All earnings exclude tips.) Dining room and cafeteria attendants earned a median of $7.10 per hour, which is approximately $14,768 per year for full-time work. The lowest paid 10 percent earned less than $5.68 per hour, or approximately $11,814 annually. Most of these attendants' earnings come from wages, while a portion may come from tip pools that are shared with other members of the wait staff. Hosts and hostesses made a median of $7.52 per hour in 2004. This makes for an approximate yearly income of $15,642. Many hosts' and hostesses' earnings come from wages, but some may share in a tip pool with other dining room workers. Counter attendants at coffee shops, cafeterias, and other such establishments earned a median hourly wage of $7.53, or approximately $15,662 annually.

Another reason earnings vary so widely in this industry is because special laws govern the minimum wage that must be paid to tipped workers. While the federal minimum wage was $5.15 at the time of writing, employers under certain circumstances are allowed to pay tipped workers less than this amount. In 2006 the minimum an employer could pay tipped workers was $2.13 per hour. The yearly income for a full-time worker making this amount is approximately $4,430 without tips.

As a benefit, most businesses offer free or discounted meals to workers. Full-time workers often receive some benefits, such as health insurance and sick days.

WORK ENVIRONMENT

Working conditions for food service workers have improved greatly, as more restaurants have been air-conditioned and modernized and many laborsaving techniques have become available. This occupational group is still subject to certain work hazards, however. These may include burns from heat and steam; cuts and injuries from knives, glassware, and other equipment; and sometimes hard falls from rushing on slippery floors. The job also requires lifting heavy trays of food, dishes, and water glasses, as well as a great deal of bending and stooping. In some cases, employees may work near steam tables or hot ovens.

Working hours will vary with the place of employment. The majority of waiters work 40- to 48-hour weeks, while food counter workers, waiters' assistants, and kitchen helpers generally work fewer than 30 hours a week. Split shifts are common to cover rush hours; some employees may work the lunch and dinner shifts, for example, with a few hours off in between. This is good for students, of course, who can then plan their courses around work schedules.

Most food service workers have to work evenings, weekends, and holidays. Some holiday work may be rotated among all the employees. One day off per week is usually in the schedule. Benefits for food service workers usually include free or discounted meals during the hours when they work. Their place of employment often furnishes work uniforms.

Work in this field is physically strenuous, requiring long hours of standing and walking, carrying heavy trays or pots and pans, and lifting other types of equipment. Rush hours are hectic, particularly for those employees who serve the public, attending to several tables or customers at the same time. Hard-to-please customers can also add to the employee's stress level.

The operation of a restaurant or other food service depends on the teamwork of its employees. An even disposition and a sense of humor, especially under pressure, contribute greatly to the efficiency and pleasantness of the restaurant's operation. The ability to converse easily with customers is a major asset for those working directly with the public.

OUTLOOK

Because work schedules can be flexible, part-time work is often available, and because people need little or no training to do this work, the food service industry employs a substantial number of people. Additionally, the demand for restaurants and other eateries continues to grow as our population grows. In particular, the large and growing population of senior citizens, who often prefer to dine at restaurants offering table service from waiters, should mean a steady demand for those in this field. According to the U.S. Department of Labor, the overall outlook for those in food service should be about as fast as the average through 2014.

Many job openings will come from the need to replace workers who have left the field. Turnover is high in these jobs for a number of reasons, including the low pay, the long hours, and the large number of students and others who do this work on a temporary basis before moving on to other occupations. Some food service workers look for seasonal job opportunities in summer or winter resort areas. They may prefer to move with the seasonal trade because they can take advantage of the benefits the vacation area offers.

Jobs for beginning workers will be more plentiful in lower-priced restaurants, where employees usually work only a short time. More expensive and formal restaurants tend to hire only experienced workers. Because of the higher pay, better tips, and other benefits, the job turnover rate is lower in these establishments, which increases the competition for job openings.

The health of the economy and some world events also affect the health of this industry. In economic downturns, people tend to eat out less frequently and go to less expensive restaurants. Some events, such as the Olympics, can draw many visitors to an area and cause a small boom for eating establishments there. Other events, such as the threat of terrorism, can cause people in that area to dine out less frequently for a time. Both such positive and negative events, however, generally have only a short-term effect on the industry.

FOR MORE INFORMATION

For information on job opportunities and accredited education programs, contact

International Council on Hotel, Restaurant, and Institutional Education
2810 North Parham Road, Suite 230
Richmond, VA 23294

Tel: 804-346-4800
http://chrie.org

For information on education, scholarships, and careers, contact
National Restaurant Association Educational Foundation
175 West Jackson Boulevard, Suite 1500
Chicago, IL 60604-2814
Tel: 800-765-2122
http://www.nraef.org

For information on food service careers and programs in Canada, contact the following associations:
Canadian Restaurant and Foodservices Association
316 Bloor Street West
Toronto, ON M5S 1W5 Canada
Tel: 800-387-5649
Email: info@crfa.ca
http://www.crfa.ca

Canadian Society of Nutrition Management
PO Box 948
Oshawa, ON L1H 1G5 Canada
Tel: 905-728-0429
Email: csnm@bellnet.ca
http://www.csnm.org

Hotel and Motel Managers

OVERVIEW

Hotel and motel managers, sometimes called *lodging managers,* are ultimately responsible for the business of running their hotel or motel smoothly and efficiently. Larger establishments may have several managers accountable for different departments. In turn, these departmental managers report to the general manager. The general manager's many duties include managing personnel, financial operations, and promotional activities. Lodging managers hold approximately 58,000 jobs in the United States.

HISTORY

As travel became more frequent in the United States and around the world, the idea of a comfortable place for travelers to stay and rest became a reality. The earliest lodging places were probably simple shelters with no food or running water available. Better roads and means of transportation allowed more people the luxury of travel, which in turn raised the standard of lodging. The early inns, called mansiones, were often located along roads. They offered a bed and, sometimes, a meal. The first hotel and motel managers were the owners themselves. They were responsible for maintaining the rooms, collecting payment, and providing food and drink to guests.

As hotels and motels began to consolidate, and chains were built, managers became more important. Many times, a single person, or family, would own numerous hotel or motel properties, and hire reliable people to help manage the business. Managers were trusted

QUICK FACTS

School Subjects
Business
Mathematics
Speech

Personal Skills
Helping/teaching
Leadership/management

Work Environment
Primarily indoors
Primarily one location

Minimum Education Level
Associate's degree

Salary Range
$20,400 to $33,970 to
$59,420+

Certification or Licensing
Voluntary

Outlook
About as fast as the average

DOT
187

GOE
11.01.01

NOC
0632

O*NET-SOC
11-9081.00

to run the establishments properly, turn a profit, and make sure rooms were filled.

THE JOB

Hotel and motel managers are responsible for the overall supervision of their establishment, the different departments, and their staff. They follow operating guidelines set by the owners, or if part of a chain, by the main headquarters and executive board. A *general manager,* often abbreviated to *GM,* allocates funds to all departments, approves expenditures, sets room rates, and establishes standards for food and beverage service, decor, and all guest services. GMs tour their property every day, usually with the head of the housekeeping department, to make certain everything is clean and orderly. GMs are responsible for keeping their establishment's accounting books in order, doing or approving the advertising and marketing, maintaining and ordering supplies, and interviewing and training new employees. However, in large hotels and motels, the GM is usually supported by one or more assistants and departmental managers.

Some hotels and motels still employ *resident managers,* who live on the premises and are on call 24 hours a day, in case of emergencies. Resident managers work regular eight-hour shifts daily, attending to the duties of the hotel or motel. In many modern establishments, the general manager has replaced the resident manager.

In large hotels and motels, departmental managers include the following.

Front office managers supervise the activity and staff of the front desk. They direct reservations and sleeping room assignments. Front office managers make sure that all guests are treated courteously and check-in and check-out periods are managed smoothly. Any guest complaints or problems are usually directed to the front desk first—front office managers are responsible for rectifying all customer complaints before they reach the general manager.

Executive housekeepers are managers who supervise the work of the room attendants, housekeepers, janitors, gardeners, and the laundry staff. Depending on the size and structure of the hotel, they may also be in charge of ordering cleaning supplies, linens, towels, and toiletries. Some executive housekeepers may be responsible for dealing with suppliers and vendors.

Personnel managers head human resources or personnel departments. They hire and fire employees and work with other personnel employees such as *training managers, benefits coordinators*, and *employee relations managers.*

Training managers oversee the hotel's management training program. Other employees in this department include benefits coordinators, who handle employee benefits such as health insurance and pension plans, and employee relations managers, who deal with employee rights and grievances with an overall goal of creating a positive and productive work atmosphere.

A *security manager,* sometimes known as a *director of hotel security,* is entrusted with the protection of the guests, workers, and grounds and property of the hotel.

Food and beverage managers are responsible for all food service operations in the hotel—from restaurants, cocktail lounges and banquets to room service. They supervise food and service quality and preparation, order supplies from different vendors, and estimate food costs.

Restaurant managers oversee the daily operation of hotel or motel restaurants. They manage employees such as waiters, buspersons, hosts, bartenders, and cooks and bakers. They also resolve customer complaints.

Large hotels and motels can profit by marketing their facilities for conventions, meetings, and special events. *Convention services managers* are in charge of coordinating such activities. The convention services manager takes care of all necessary details, such as blocking sleeping rooms for the group, arranging for meeting rooms or ballrooms, and resolving any problems that arise.

Hotel chains employ specialized managers to ensure that its hotels are being operated appropriately and in a financially sound manner. *Regional operations managers* travel throughout a specific geographic region to see that hotel chain members are operated and maintained according to the guidelines and standards set by the company. *Branch operations managers* reorganize hotels that are doing poorly financially, or set up a new hotel operation.

REQUIREMENTS

High School

It's a good idea to begin preparing for a career in hotel management while in high school. Concentrate on a business-oriented curriculum, with classes in finance, accounting, and mathematics. Since computers are widely used in the hotel setting for reservations, accounting, and management of supplies, it is important that you become computer literate. Brush up on your communication skills while in high school. You'll need them when giving direction and supervision to a large and diverse staff. Take English classes and other courses, such as speech or drama, that will give you the chance to polish your grammar and speaking skills. A second language, especially Spanish, French, or Japanese, will be very helpful to you in the future.

Postsecondary Training

While you should be able to get a starting position at a hotel or motel with only a high school diploma, many companies now require management trainees to have a minimum of a bachelor's degree in hotel and restaurant management. Numerous community and junior colleges and some universities offer associate's, bachelor's, or graduate degree programs in hotel or restaurant management. In addition, technical, vocational, and trade schools and other institutions offer hotel business programs resulting in a formal recognition of training, such as a certificate.

Classes in hotel management cover topics such as administration, marketing, housekeeping, hotel maintenance, and computer skills. To complement class instruction, most programs require students to work on site at a hotel.

Many hotels and motels will also consider candidates with liberal arts degrees or degrees in such fields as business management and public relations if they are highly qualified and talented.

Certification or Licensing

Certification for this job is not a requirement, though it is recognized by many as a measurement of industry knowledge and job experience. The Educational Institute of the American Hotel and Lodging Association offers a variety of certifications for hotel and motel managers, including certified hotel administrator, certified lodging manager, certified lodging security director, certified food and beverage executive, certified hospitality housekeeping executive, certified human resources executive, certified engineering operations executive, certified hospitality supervisor, and certified lodging security supervisor. Contact the Institute for more information on these certifications.

High school juniors and seniors who are interested in working in the hospitality industry can take advantage of the *Educational Institute of the American Hotel and Lodging Association's* Lodging Management Program. The program combines classroom learning with work experience in the hospitality industry. Graduating seniors who pass examinations and work in the lodging industry for at least 30 days receive the certified rooms division specialist designation. Visit http://www.lodgingmanagement for more information.

Other Requirements

Managers are strong leaders who have a flair for organization and communication and, most important, work well with all types of people. To keep the hotel or motel running smoothly, general managers need to establish policies and procedures and make certain their directions are followed. Managing can sometimes be stressful, and managers need to keep a cool demeanor when dealing with difficult situations that come their way.

Vlato Lemick, general manager and owner of several hotels in the Chicago area, considers dealing with customer complaints to be one of his most challenging job duties. "Problems do reach my desk, and I have to take care of them." Does he only give attention to the important problems? "No," he says firmly. "No complaint or request should be considered unimportant."

EXPLORING

You can test your interest in this career firsthand by visiting a local hotel or motel and spending a day at the front desk, or better yet, with the general manager. Most high schools have a job shadowing program that introduces students to various careers. If your school doesn't have such a program, talk with your counseling center about implementing one.

Working in hospitality is really the best way to explore the field. Part-time jobs in any department, no matter how small, will give you important business experience. Here's a success story to inspire you. Keith Pierce's first hotel job was loading dishwashers at the Waldorf Astoria. Many dishes later, armed with a college degree and work experience, Pierce was promoted to vice president of Wingate Hotels.

EMPLOYERS

There are approximately 58,000 hotel and motel managers working in the United States. Half of these workers own their own hotel or motel.

Some major employers in the industry are Cendant Corporation (Days Inn, Super 8, Ramada, Howard Johnson, Travelodge), Inter-Continental Hotels Group (Holiday Inn), and VIP International Corporation. These companies have properties located nationwide and abroad. Host Marriott Corporation, another international player, offers a fast-track management program for qualified employees and has been known to encourage career advancement for minorities and women.

Long-term experience is important in this industry. It is wise to work at least one year at a company before moving to another. Employers are likely to question applicants who have had more than four employers in less than two years.

STARTING OUT

The position of general manager is one of the top rungs on this career ladder. It's unlikely this would be your first industry job. In today's highly technical age, experience, though still important, is not enough for job advancement. Most candidates have some postsecondary education; many have at least a bachelor's degree in hotel and restaurant management. Graduates entering the hotel industry usually pay their dues by working as assistant managers, assistant departmental managers, or shift managers. Many hotels and motels have specific management training programs for their management-bound employees. Employees are encouraged to work different desks so they will be knowledgeable about each department.

Your school's career center, the local library, and the Internet can all be helpful when researching college programs or specific businesses.

ADVANCEMENT

The average tenure of a general manager is between six and seven years; those who have worked as a GM for 10 years or more usually view their job as a lifetime commitment. Managers who leave the profession usually advance to the regional or even national area of hotel and motel management, such as property management or the administrative or financial departments of the lodging chain. Some may opt to open their own hotel or motel franchises or even operate a small inn or bed and breakfast. The management skills learned as a general manager can be successfully utilized in any avenue of business.

EARNINGS

Salary figures vary according to the worker's level of expertise, the lodging establishment, the duties involved, the size of the hotel or motel, and its location. General managers working in large urban areas can expect to have more responsibilities and higher compensation than those at smaller inns in rural areas.

According to the U.S. Department of Labor, lodging managers reported a median yearly income of $37,660 in 2004. The lowest paid 10 percent earned less than $22,680 annually, and the highest paid 10 percent made more than $72,160 per year. Managers may receive bonuses of 20 to 25 percent of their base salary when conditions are favorable, such as during a strong economy and when managers have increased business. These bonuses can often boost earnings by thousands of dollars.

Managers receive paid vacation and sick days and other benefits, such as medical and life insurance, and pension or profit-sharing plans. They may also receive free or discounted lodging, meals, parking, and laundry, as well as financial assistance with education.

WORK ENVIRONMENT

Don't expect to manage a 200-room hotel sitting behind a desk. General managers make at least one property walk-through a day, inspecting the condition of the hotel. The rest of the day is spent returning phone calls, meeting with clients, and running from one department to another. Managers do not have nine-to-five days; they usually work an average of 55 hours a week. Weekends and holidays are no exceptions. Off-duty managers are sometimes called back to work in cases of emergency—night or day—and they don't go home until the problem is solved. Managers interact with many different people, such as hotel or motel staff, tourists in town to see the sights, business people attending conventions, and numerous other professionals in the hospitality industry. Not everyone is polite or reasonable, and managers must be able to "think on their feet" and work calmly in difficult situations.

OUTLOOK

Overall, the employment outlook for lodging managers is predicted to grow about as fast as the average through 2014, according to the U.S. Department of Labor. Vacancies will occur as hotel and motel managers change jobs and careers. (The long hours and constant demands of this career often result in career changes.) In addition, as the number of business and leisure travelers continues to increase, the demand for more economy-class rooms, extended-stay hotels, and suite hotels, which offer suites with apartment-like features such as kitchens, should rise. The continuing popularity of large full-service hotels with specialized offerings such as child-care centers, several restaurants, business meeting facilities, and fitness centers will also provide ample opportunities for hotel and motel managers. In general, job candidates with college degrees in hotel and motel management will be highly sought after.

FOR MORE INFORMATION

For information on careers in hotel management, contact
American Hotel and Lodging Association
1201 New York Avenue, NW, Suite 600

Washington, DC 20005-3931
Tel: 202-289-3100
Email: info@ahla.com
http://www.ahma.com

For information on internships, scholarships, and certification requirements, contact
Educational Institute of the American Hotel and Lodging Association
800 North Magnolia Avenue, Suite 1800
Orlando, FL 32803
Tel: 407-999-8100
Email: info@ei-ahla.org
http://www.ei-ahla.org

For information and a listing of hostels worldwide, contact
Hosteling International USA
8401 Colesville Road, Suite 600
Silver Spring, MD 20910
Tel: 301-495-1240
http://www.hiayh.org

For information on sales and marketing careers in hospitality, contact
Hospitality Sales and Marketing Association International
8201 Greensboro Drive, Suite 300
McLean, VA 22102
Tel: 703-610-9024
http://www.hsmai.org

For education information and a list of available school programs, contact
International Council on Hotel, Restaurant and Institutional Education
2810 North Parham Road, Suite 203
Richmond, VA 23294
Tel: 804-346-4800
http://chrie.org

Hotel Concierges

OVERVIEW

Concierges assist hotel guests and help make their stays pleasant and comfortable. Guests may use their services to book tours, airline reservations, or car rentals. Concierges are experts in what their particular city has to offer. Many times they may be asked to recommend restaurants, shows, or museums as well as give directions to other points of interest. Concierges may also be asked to plan cocktail receptions, dinner meetings, or small parties for hotel guests. There are approximately 18,000 concierges employed in the United States.

HISTORY

Concierges have been around since the Middle Ages. The word *concierge* comes from the Latin term *conservus,* meaning "fellow slave." In the past, trusted slaves were trained to assist their owners, often traveling ahead to make sure accommodations and food were in order. Holding the keys to the castle, these slaves became doorkeepers; they were relied upon to make sure everyone was safely locked in for the night. Throughout the years, as luxury hotels were built across Europe, it was necessary to install concierges to provide the same type of service for their guests. It was not until the mid-1970s that American hotels realized the need for the services of a concierge. Today, most hotels maintain a concierge department relative to the property's size and number of guests.

THE JOB

Concierges are the most visible and active ambassadors of hotel hospitality. Their basic duty is to provide hotel guests with services to help make their stay as comfortable, enjoyable, and memorable as possible. Many of the requests concierges receive are for directions to city attractions, recommendations for tours or restaurants, or help dealing with airlines or car rental agencies. Concierges obtain out-of-town newspapers, arrange for the pickup of dry cleaning, or reserve show tickets. Concierges also work with other departments in the hotel to prepare for large groups, VIP guests, or any guest that may have special needs. Sometimes welcome letters or baskets of fruit are sent to such guests by the concierge desk. However, concierge duties do not end there. Many hotels provide different levels of concierge service, depending on the type of guest. Penthouse guests can enjoy a private reception with a separate concierge department to meet their needs as well as serve them afternoon tea and hot hors d'oeuvres and drinks during the cocktail hour. Some concierge desks also host similar cocktail hours in the lobby.

Sometimes, a request can be more involved. Concierges have been known to plan large dinners or receptions on short notice, design entire travel itineraries complete with lodging and tours, rent airplanes or helicopters, secure the front row seats to a sold-out concert or sporting event, or even fill a room with flowers to set the mood for a marriage proposal. Concierges are trained to use their resources and contacts to serve the guest in whatever manner possible. They will, however, refuse to help the guest in any acts unlawful or unkind—no illegal drugs, prostitution, or practical jokes that may be deemed hurtful.

Concierges also spend a considerable amount of time researching restaurants, tours, museums, and other city attractions. Since a recommendation can bring additional business, many tour operators will pay special attention to visiting concierges.

REQUIREMENTS

High School

A well-rounded high school education is a good starting point for the career of concierge. Speech and writing classes will help you learn how to effectively communicate with hotel guests and coworkers. Fluency in another language, especially French, Japanese, or Spanish, can also be extremely helpful in this field.

Postsecondary Training

A college degree is not required to be a concierge. In fact, many successful and established concierges have a variety of educational and employment backgrounds—from managers to artists to teachers.

However, in today's competitive job market it pays to have an edge. A well-rounded education, such as a liberal arts degree or a degree from a concierge program, could only help.

Certification or Licensing
Though not a requirement, certification is viewed by many as a measurement of professional achievement. The Educational Institute of the American Hotel and Lodging Association offers certification classes for concierges. The National Concierge Association (NCA) offers certification to members who meet educational, experience, and organization activity level requirements. Only one program, however, is directly involved with the Les Clefs d'Or organization—the International Concierge Institute (ICI). ICI, in partnership with the International School of Tourism, offers training and certification courses on tourism and hotel trends, guest service, human relations, concierge behavior, and protocol, as well as a required language program. The National Concierge Association also offers certification to qualified concierges.

High school juniors and seniors who are interested in working in the hospitality industry can take advantage of the *Educational Institute of the American Hotel and Lodging Association's* Lodging Management Program. The program combines classroom learning with work experience in the hospitality industry. Graduating seniors who pass examinations and work in the lodging industry for at least 30 days receive the certified rooms division specialist designation. Visit http://www.lodgingmanagement.org for more information.

Other Requirements
Decorum is a key word in this industry. A good concierge is always well-groomed and dressed neatly. No matter how difficult the situation, concierges should always be polite and pleasant. They never gossip about the guests. If a guest has a strange request, the concierge should always be very discreet so as not to embarrass the guest or the hotel.

What separates an adequate concierge from a great one? "What you look for in a concierge," offers Diana Nelson, chief concierge at San Francisco's Grand Hyatt Hotel, "is an attitude. It's the feeling someone has in making a difference in a person's stay."

EXPLORING
Try to find part-time or seasonal work in order to gain working experience. Your part-time job need not be in a hotel (although

that's the best place to make contacts); consider working in the customer service department of a department store. What about working as a junior assistant for a wedding consultant or party caterer? If you are always recruited to show out-of-town relatives the city sights, then at least get paid for your efforts by working for a tour company.

EMPLOYERS

Look for jobs in large cities like New York, Los Angeles, and Chicago; tourist-heavy areas, such as California and Florida; and the convention and entertainment mecca of Las Vegas. Employment opportunities are plentiful abroad, although European standards and training may be different from those found in the United States (check with the ICI).

Concierges also work in other aspects of business. Besides hotels, concierges work in some large apartment buildings and condominiums. The concierge services provided at one Chicago high-rise apartment building include taking clothes to the cleaners, watering plants, and caring for pets when occupants are out of town. Large upscale department stores, such as Nordstrom, offer concierge services for their shoppers, from complimentary coat and package checking to restaurant and store information and tours.

STARTING OUT

At most hotels, new hires are not allowed to sit at the lobby desk until they are properly trained. The first few days are spent going over the basic philosophy of being a concierge and the hotel's expectations of employees. Many concierge trainees come from other departments of the hotel, such as the front desk. Diana Nelson likes to start trainees in the Regency Club, a special service provided by the Grand Hyatt to their VIP guests. Here special guests can relax and be served gourmet food and drinks. The pace in the Regency Club is slower, but expectations are high when it comes to service because of the clientele; this makes a great training ground before concierges are allowed to work the lobby, where according to Nelson, "you almost have to be able to do three or four things at the same time—with a lot of ease."

There is no typical path to this career. Some concierges have only a high school education. Being a graduate of a hotel or concierge program will, however, give you an edge in getting hired. Many schools with such programs, such as ICI, offer job placement services. Also,

The Magic Bag

A good concierge can anticipate guests' needs by having the following supplies well-stocked and readily available. Here are some examples of items found in a concierge's "magic bag" of supplies:

- ties and cufflinks
- scissors
- wrapping paper
- ribbons
- candles
- voltage converters

- umbrellas
- black socks
- clear nail polish
- lint brushes
- medical kits
- postage stamps

check hotel industry publications as they often post employment opportunities. Les Clefs d'Or takes great pride in the worldwide networking program it provides its members.

ADVANCEMENT

There are many opportunities for concierges who want to advance to other hotel departments. Because a concierge's duties are very people-oriented, similar positions, such as front desk manager, should be considered. A concierge who has a degree in hotel management or business, and work experience, as well as superior management skills, could vie for the position of general manager.

The extremely ambitious can also start their own concierge businesses. *Personal concierges* are personal assistants to those too busy to organize their homes or run errands. For a fixed price, known as a *retainer,* personal concierges are responsible for a set of weekly duties; special requests, such as planning dinner parties or buying Christmas gifts, are charged extra.

EARNINGS

The U.S. Department of Labor reports that concierges earned salaries that ranged from less than $15,500 to $35,000 or more in 2004, with median annual earnings of $23,500. An experienced concierge, with Les Clefs d'Or status, working at a large urban hotel, can expect to earn around $50,000 a year, according to ICI. Concierges employed by hotels typically receive benefits such as paid vacations, sick and holiday time, health insurance, and some type of employee hotel discount, depending on the establishment.

Concierge service is a free service provided to the guests by the hotel. A concierge, especially a good one, is often given tips or gifts by grateful hotel patrons. Concierges, ethically, cannot and will not press for tips. The hotel guest decides whether to tip, and if so, how much.

WORK ENVIRONMENT

Most concierges have workstations, usually a desk or a counter, prominently situated in the main lobby. Concierges spend much of the day on their feet, greeting guests, making phone calls, running errands, or doing whatever it takes to make things happen. A considerable amount of time is spent in the field, trying out new restaurants, visiting museums, and researching new tours. Concierges need to be up on what's new and happening in their city. Flexibility is imperative in this job since there is no such thing as "a typical day." A good concierge must be ready to deal with a single guest or a group of 20, always in a cheerful and courteous manner. Situations can get hectic, especially when it's the middle of the tourist season or the hotel is full of conventioneers.

OUTLOOK

Job opportunities look bright for those interested in a concierge career. Busier lifestyles leave little time for mundane chores or last-minute details. Once shy of or intimidated by the concierge desk, savvy travelers now realize this is a free service available for their convenience. Some hotels have experimented with computerized kiosks advertising tours and restaurants. These displays are less personal, however, and since listings are in essence a paid advertisement, they do not provide a true recommendation. Hotel general managers realize that a concierge department can provide the ultimate in guest services; and it is that type of service that makes a hotel a true luxury hotel. Even many smaller hotels, especially those that cater to business travelers, are now providing concierge service.

The hotel industry has been affected by the struggling economy and recent terrorist activity. The number of travelers has decreased, and the industry does not expect a full recovery for several years. Because concierges provide a valuable public relations service for their hotels, their jobs are not likely to be affected. The best hotels will look for concierges with experience, membership in an organization like Les Clefs d'Or, and connections with people in local restaurants, transportation companies, special events organizations, and tourism councils.

FOR MORE INFORMATION

For information on hotel careers, contact
  American Hotel and Lodging Association
  1201 New York Avenue, NW, Suite 600
  Washington, DC 20005-3931
  Tel: 202-289-3100
  Email: info@ahla.com
  http://www.ahma.com

For information on internships, scholarships, or certification requirements, contact
  Educational Institute of the American Hotel and Lodging Association
  800 North Magnolia Avenue, Suite 1800
  Orlando, FL 32803
  Tel: 800-752-4567
  Email: info@ei-ahla.org
  http://www.ei-ahla.org

For more information on concierge careers and opportunities, contact
  Les Clefs d'Or USA
  24088 North Bridle Trail Road
  Lake Forest, IL 60045
  http://lcdusa.org

For information on local chapters, certification, and publications, contact
  National Concierge Association
  Tel: 612-317-2932
  Email: info@nationalconciergeassociation.com
  http://www.nationalconciergeassociation.com/

Hotel Desk Clerks

OVERVIEW

Hotel desk clerks work the front desk and are responsible for performing a variety of services, such as registering guests, assigning rooms, and providing general information. For many guests, the front desk worker gives them their first impression of the hotel. There are about 195,000 desk clerks employed at lodging properties, large and small, in the United States.

HISTORY

The very first desk clerks were simply the owners of a lodging establishment or members of their family. Besides managing the inn, cleaning the rooms, and cooking the food, the innkeepers were responsible for assigning rooms and collecting fees. As hotels grew bigger, many consolidated to create chains, such as the Statler Hotels or Holiday Inn. Sometimes a single owner was responsible for a number of properties. Innkeepers realized they needed help from employees apart from their immediate families. Desk clerks were trusted to manage the duties of the front desk—welcoming guests, assigning rooms, and maintaining hotel records.

Today, front office workers use computers to reduce paperwork, keep better records, and manage reservation systems. New software is constantly being developed to help the front office. For example, the Front Desk Resort Management System updates the master registry book by keeping track of reservations and guest information. Many guests now opt to use the in-room video express or telephone checkout instead of waiting in line. Even with such technological advancements, desk clerks are still needed to staff the front desk.

Guests like personal attention to certain details such as answering their questions and handling special requests. Desk clerks process video checkouts, as well, and then mail folios to guests.

THE JOB

The duties of the desk clerk can be separated into four categories: process reservations, register the guest, serve as primary guest liaison, and process guest departure.

Process reservations. Desk clerks, or more specifically, *reservation clerks,* handle the duties of guest reservations, most often over the phone. They determine if the requested date is available, quote rates, record advance deposits or prepayments, confirm room reservations, and describe policies and services to guests. Reservation clerks, when dealing with reservation discrepancies, may have to retrieve hotel records or change or cancel the reservation to resolve the problem to the guest's satisfaction. Reservation clerks must also analyze the guest's special needs while at the hotel and relay them to the proper department.

Register the guest. After greeting the guest, desk clerks obtain and verify the required registration information, such as the guest's name, address, and length of stay. A credit card is usually required as a deposit or guarantee. Once the paperwork is done, room keys or key cards are issued, and guests are directed to their rooms.

Serve as primary guest liaison. Desk clerks often act as a buffer between the hotel and the guest. When guests have problems, have special requests, or encounter difficulties, they usually turn to the most visible person for help—the desk clerk. Some services provided to guests are laundry and valet requests, wake-up calls, and delivery of mail or messages. Clerks may also provide general information regarding the hotel or surrounding community. Their most important task, however, is to quickly address requests and complaints or to redirect the guest to the proper department.

Process guest departures. In some lodging establishments, a guest can choose to settle his or her account while in the room via the express video or telephone checkout. Room charges are tallied and charged to the customer's credit card. Desk clerks settle video and telephone checkouts at the end of the day and send folios to the guest's home address. However, many people still choose to personally check out at the front desk. After verifying and explaining all room charges, the desk clerk can begin to settle the guest's account. Sometimes, if credit authorization is declined, the clerk may have to politely negotiate an alternate method of payment. After thanking the guest and listening to any comments, positive or negative, the desk clerk can move on to the next customer or task.

Front office workers are responsible for keeping the hotel's information systems up-to-date. Many hotels now keep detailed information on their guests, such as the reason for their stay and their likes and dislikes. They use this information for future marketing needs. Depending on the type or size of the hotel, they may also be responsible for working the switchboard, bookkeeping, house banks and petty cash, daily bank deposits, and recoding key cards. In addition, they must keep the front desk area clean and presentable.

REQUIREMENTS

High School

High school classes can be a useful foundation for a career in the hotel industry. Concentrate on classes such as human relations, business or marketing, and even sociology to prepare yourself for this people-oriented job. Be sure to take English and speech courses to hone your communications skills. Lynda Witry, front desk supervisor at the Giorgios Hotel and Conference Center in Orland Park, Illinois, found her high school computer and typing classes helpful. "Being able to type—not the hunt-and-peck method—makes working on the computer faster." According to Witry, it helps to know how to compute percentages and discounts, so be sure to take math courses.

Postsecondary Training

If you are hoping to use a desk clerk job as a stepping-stone to a management position, you should seriously consider a degree in hotel management. College courses that will be helpful to your career include human relations, finance, and practical classes, such as hospitality supervision and front office procedures.

Internships are a great way to earn work experience, course credit, and most important, a chance to distinguish yourself from other applicants come interview time. Check with your high school guidance counselor or career center for a listing of available hospitality internships and schools that have two- or four-year programs, or contact the Educational Institute of the American Hotel and Lodging Association.

Certification or Licensing

Certification is not a requirement for the position of desk clerk, though it is considered by many as a measure of industry knowledge and experience. Programs, such as those offered by the Educational Institute of the American Hotel and Lodging Association, are designed to help improve job performance and advancement potential and keep you up-to-date on industry changes.

High school juniors and seniors who are interested in working in the hospitality industry can take advantage of the *Educational Institute of the American Hotel and Lodging Association's Lodging* Management Program. The program combines classroom learning with work experience in the hospitality industry. Graduating seniors who pass examinations and work in the lodging industry for at least 30 days receive the certified rooms division specialist designation. Visit http://www.lodgingmanagement.org for more information.

Other Requirements

"Desk clerks should be great communicators," says Witry. "They need to be able to deal with different kinds of people to be successful in this job." Organization, flexibility, and patience are some qualities needed when handling different situations and tasks simultaneously. You should be courteous and eager to help, even at times when the guests are demanding. When unable to help, you must be able to relay the guests' demands to the proper department. As a desk clerk, you will spend the majority of the day on your feet, so you should be in good physical condition. Computer knowledge, good phone manners, and readable penmanship are desirable for this job. Fluency in other languages, though not a requirement, is a great plus.

Good grooming habits are essential for this high-visibility job. Strive for a professional look. Industry no-nos include "big hair," excessive jewelry, and heavy or dramatic makeup. Desk clerks usually wear uniforms provided by the hotel that are cleaned free of charge at some hotels.

EXPLORING

The best way to explore this industry is to work in a hotel after school or during summer vacations. Although you may not land a desk clerk position, you may be hired as a waiter, waitress, dining-room attendant, or a housekeeping position. You will be able to talk to people in the industry and learn the pros and cons of each job. If you can't find a job in the hotel industry, you might consider asking your guidance counselor to arrange an information interview with someone working in the field.

EMPLOYERS

Approximately 195,000 hotel, motel, and resort desk clerks are employed in the United States. Because hotels and motels are found worldwide, job opportunities for desk clerks are plentiful. The amount of responsibility given to a desk clerk depends on the size and type of lodging establishment. Larger hotels (usually located in busy urban areas), such as the 650-room Sheraton Manhattan in New York, may have separate departments, each responsible for answering phones, making advance reservations, or processing guest arrivals. The pace of work may be more frenzied at times because of the higher guest count. The Crowne Plaza in Indianapolis, Indiana, a smaller hotel, may have to combine departments to accommodate a smaller staff.

STARTING OUT

Many jobs are posted in newspaper want ads, trade magazines, or hotel employee newsletters. Hoteljobs.com (http://www.hoteljobs.com) is a website where you can post your resume and search for jobs nationwide. High school job centers and their counselors are helpful in providing guidance, handbooks, and literature to interested students. They may even post part-time or seasonal work available in the field.

Hiring requirements vary from employer to employer, but most hotels look for candidates with work experience as well as education. Many desk clerks have a high school diploma or the equivalent; but those ambitious enough to someday run the management track should consider obtaining an associate's or bachelor's degree in hotel management or a similar program. When applying for a job, experience in the hotel industry is a definite plus, though experience in the restaurant trade, customer service, or retail is equally valuable.

ADVANCEMENT

Desk clerks and reservation clerks are both considered entry-level positions. Promotions within the front office could lead to jobs as front desk supervisor or front office manager. Further advancement may be to the position of assistant hotel manager. It is also possible to move to other departments within the hotel, such as banquets or the sales department. Job promotions, especially to the management level, will be easier to obtain with further education.

EARNINGS

According to the U.S. Department of Labor, median annual earnings of hotel, motel, and resort desk clerks were $17,700 in 2004. The lowest paid 10 percent of these workers earned $13,040 or less per year, while the highest paid 10 percent made $25,200 or more annually. Salaries depend on the size, type, and location of the hotel.

After a probationary period, usually 90 days, hotel desk clerks are frequently offered medical and sometimes dental insurance, vacation and sick days, paid holidays, and employee discounts. Many companies offer employees several free nights' stay per year at any of their properties.

WORK ENVIRONMENT

The front desk is located inside the hotel lobby, which is often clean and well decorated for the benefit of the guests. Desk clerks are on their feet most of the day, greeting guests and processing the paperwork needed for check-ins and check-outs. Most full-time desk clerks work a normal eight-hour day. However, because hotels are open 24 hours a day, it may be necessary for new employees with little seniority to work less-desirable shifts. Some holiday work should be expected.

This industry, as a rule, tends to have a high turnover rate. Larger hotels, especially those located in busy urban areas, may offer faster opportunities for advancement. Job openings are created as people climb the corporate ladder or leave the workforce for other reasons.

OUTLOOK

According to the *Occupational Outlook Handbook,* employment of hotel desk clerks is expected to grow about as fast as the average through 2014. There has been an increase in business and personal travel in the past few years, and this trend is expected to continue. In addition, travel trends indicate that many people are taking several shorter, long-weekend vacations several times a year instead of one big trip. This type of travel increases the number of nights spent in hotel rooms, which promotes job growth within the hotel industry. Since there is a high rate of turnover in this field, new hotel and motel desk clerks are always needed to replace those who vacate their positions.

Jobs will be most plentiful with hotels located in busy urban areas, where there tend to be higher turnover rates. Opportunities will also be good at extended-stay and budget hotels. Hotel desk clerks at these facilities are generally responsible for a wider range of duties, such as business and concierge-related services.

Most skills needed to be a good desk clerk are learned on the job. On-site training is a common method of continuing education, though hotels may choose to send their management-track employees to off-site seminars or continuing education classes.

FOR MORE INFORMATION

For information on the hotel industry, career opportunities, and scholarships, contact the following organizations:

American Hotel and Lodging Association
1201 New York Avenue, NW, Suite 600
Washington, DC 20005-3931
Tel: 202-289-3100
Email: info@ahla.com
http://www.ahma.com

For career and certification information, contact

Educational Institute of the American Hotel and Lodging Association
800 North Magnolia Avenue, Suite 1800
Orlando, FL 32803
Tel: 800-752-4567
Email: info@ei-ahla.org
http://www.ei-ahla.org

For a listing of schools with programs in hotel management, contact

International Council on Hotel, Restaurant & Institutional Education
2810 North Parham, Suite 230
Richmond, VA 23294-4442
Tel: 804-346-4800
http://chrie.org

Hotel Executive Housekeepers

OVERVIEW

Hotel executive housekeepers direct and control the staff and operations of housekeeping departments within a hotel. They are responsible for ensuring that the rooms and property are clean and presentable. Millions of people are employed at all levels of housekeeping and in different fields, such as lodging, hospitals, nursing homes, retail, and schools. The International Executive Housekeeping Association, an organization for housekeeping executives, has about 4,000 members.

HISTORY

A large part of any hotel's reputation rests on its appearance. A posh hotel would lose some of its grandeur if the lobby looked cluttered and dirty. Hotel patrons don't mind paying higher room fees when they are guaranteed some measure of luxury, if only for a night or two. Because all guests, whether paying $29.99 a night at the Motel 6 or $300+ a night at the Hotel Intercontinental, expect their rooms to be neat and orderly, the housekeeping staff is vital to the success of any motel or hotel. At the helm of the hotel housekeeping department is the executive housekeeper, also known as the *director of housekeeping services*.

The earliest housekeeping executives were most probably owners of the hotel. Often the innkeepers did not have any help aside from family members; they were responsible for cleaning the inn, cooking food, showing guests to their rooms, and maintaining records. Eventually, hotels became bigger, and in some cases they merged

QUICK FACTS

School Subjects
Business
Mathematics

Personal Skills
Helping/teaching
Leadership/management

Work Environment
Primarily indoors
Primarily one location

Minimum Education Level
Associate's degree

Salary Range
$22,680 to $37,660 to
$72,160

Certification or Licensing
Recommended

Outlook
About as fast as the average

DOT
187

GOE
11.01.01

NOC
6213

O*NET-SOC
11-9081.00, 37-1011.00,
37-1011.01

with other hotels to form chains and franchises. Soon, owners were forced to hire employees to help with the operations of the hotel.

This job is not defined by a mop and bucket. Executive house-keepers, one of the highest managerial positions in hospitality, are responsible for overseeing the cleanliness and appearance of the hotel. They supervise a team of cleaning professionals who keep the hotel in top condition.

Executive housekeepers need to be comfortable working with computers, a vital tool in maintaining paperwork, vendor information, and supply inventory. They also need to be familiar with new techniques to expedite the process of cleaning without sacrificing thoroughness. Robotics, for example, has helped the workload of cleaners. Much of the lifting and cleaning of heavy pieces of furniture is now done by machinery. Large lobby areas are now cleaned with automatic washers instead of hand mops. Cleaning solutions have improved to work faster and better, yet remain safe for different woods and fabrics as well as the environment.

THE JOB

The primary duty of executive housekeepers is to ensure the cleanliness of the hotel. They supervise, coordinate, and direct the activities of the hotel housekeeping department. They determine the cleaning needs of different areas in the hotel—lobby, sleeping rooms, restaurants, pools—and schedule cleaning crews accordingly. Areas are inspected regularly to make certain safety standards and departmental policies are being met. They hire and train the cleaning staff, as well as recommend promotions, transfers, and, if necessary, dismissals. Executive housekeepers are also responsible for keeping inventory of cleaning supplies and equipment, as well as hotel linens, towels, and soaps. They deal directly with vendors to learn about the latest in cleaning solutions, equipment, and techniques.

The cleaning of uniforms worn by the hotel staff, as well as all hotel laundry, is among the executive housekeepers' responsibilities. They prepare reports concerning room occupancy, department budget expenses, and employee work records for payroll. Some executive housekeepers may help decorate the hotel. Some also direct the setup for conventions and banquets.

Though executive housekeepers may share in some of the cleaning duties, in larger hotels their role is mostly administrative. Some extremely busy hotels may even hire *assistant executive housekeepers* or *assistant directors* to share in the administrative duties of keeping house. *Shift supervisors* are directly responsible for the employees

Books to Read

Casado, Matt A. *Housekeeping Management.* Hoboken, N.J.: John Wiley and Sons, 1999.

Kappa, Margaret M., Aleta Nitschke, and Patricia B. Schappert. *Managing Housekeeping Operations.* 2nd ed. Orlando, Fla.: Educational Institute of the American Hotel and Motel Association, 1997.

Martin, Robert J. *Professional Management of Housekeeping Operations.* 3d ed. Hoboken, N.J.: John Wiley and Sons, 1998.

Rutherford, Denney G. *Hotel Management and Operations.* 3d ed. Hoboken, N.J.: John Wiley and Sons, 2001.

and the work done on their particular shift. (Hotels run 24 hours a day, so many have implemented a three-shift system.) *Floor managers* and *inspectors* supervise the team of room attendants assigned to a particular floor. A *status person* handles any special requests a guest might make while at the hotel.

The cleaning staff also keep the lobby neat and orderly. They empty trash cans and ashtrays, gather glasses from the lobby tables, dust furniture, clean mirrors, and vacuum carpets and rugs. Hotel restaurants are also cleaned and maintained throughout the day. Pools and health clubs must be cleaned and sanitized. *Room attendants* are responsible for the guest rooms. They tidy sleeping rooms and bathrooms, replenish towels, soaps, shampoos, and lotions, and attend to any special requests for cribs, ironing boards, or extra supplies. They also stock and keep records of the minibar.

REQUIREMENTS

High School
Business subjects, general science, and mathematics classes will give you a solid educational foundation for working in this field. Speech and English courses will boost your communication skills.

Postsecondary Training
Though hotels recognize the importance of experience, with today's competitive market, it is increasingly important to have further education. A bachelor's degree in hotel management is your best bet, but an associate's degree is valued as well. Emphasize course work in business administration, accounting, budgeting, and economics.

Classes in communication, sociology, and psychology will prove helpful in dealing with a large, diverse staff. Other useful classes are interior design and purchasing.

Certification or Licensing

Certification or registration is not required of executive housekeepers, though it is something many seek. It is often considered a measure of professional success. The International Executive Housekeepers Association, among other institutions, offers two designations: certified executive housekeeper (CEH) and registered executive housekeeper (REH). Qualified individuals earn these designations by fulfilling educational requirements through a certificate program, a self-study program, or a college degree program.

High school juniors and seniors who are interested in working in the hospitality industry can take advantage of the *Educational Institute of the American Hotel and Lodging Association's Lodging* Management Program. The program combines classroom learning with work experience in the hospitality industry. Graduating seniors who pass examinations and work in the lodging industry for at least 30 days receive the certified rooms division specialist designation. Visit http://www.lodgingmanagement.org for more information.

Other Requirements

Executive housekeepers and their assistants need to be good communicators to keep their staffs happy and working well. Motivation is key when working with large cleaning staffs. In a pinch, good managers may help with cleaning duties. "It helps to know what is expected from all employees, at whatever level, firsthand. It gives you credibility, and respect from your staff," says Kay Wireck, executive housekeeper for Bally's Casino and Resort in Las Vegas.

As with most service-oriented jobs, customers' complaints are inevitable. "Some complaints are credible," says Wireck. "Others are not." It is the manager's job to assess the situation and resolve the problem.

EXPLORING

Try to land a job in the field. You won't be hired as an executive housekeeper, but you can land a position in the housekeeping department. This will give you a good chance to learn more about this career firsthand.

A hotel internship can give you a taste of the career without the pressures and obligations of a full-time job. Many recruiters pay more attention to former interns than to those with no past affiliation with the hotel.

EMPLOYERS

Housekeeping is needed in every industry, and positions can be found worldwide. However, jobs are clustered in urban or resort areas where there is great demand for large hotels. Larger hotels usually employ a few assistant executive housekeepers who report to the head of the housekeeping department. If you are an executive housekeeper at a smaller motel or inn, chances are your department may consist of only one or two people. Roll up your sleeves and get ready to clean!

STARTING OUT

This position is among the top rungs of the hotel corporate ladder; very few people start their hospitality careers at this level. Most college graduates start out as floor managers or supervisors and move up from there. High school graduates are usually hired for line-level jobs, such as room attendants. A college degree is not always a requirement, but without one, your climb to the top will take much longer. Check with school placement centers, newspaper want ads, and trade magazines, such as *Executive Housekeeping Today* (http://www.ieha.org/publications/publication_nav.htm), for job openings.

ADVANCEMENT

Executive housekeepers are considered part of the hotel's executive team and are on the same level as the director of food and beverages or the hotel manager. Because executive housekeepers are already at the head of their particular department, advancement possibilities are limited. Promotions are usually to other hotel departments. Kay Wireck says that she has seen many directors of housekeeping advance to higher positions such as that of general manager. "Anyone with the managerial experience of an executive housekeeper can move on." Executive housekeepers are needed in every industry where cleanliness is top priority.

EARNINGS

Overall earnings are affected by experience, level of education, type and size of organization, and number of employees supervised. The

U.S. Department of Labor reports that median annual earnings of hotel managers and assistants, a category that includes executive housekeepers, were $37,660 in 2004. Salaries ranged from less than $22,680 to more than $72,160.

As part of the salary package, managers are offered health, dental, and life insurance; pension or 401(k) plans; and hotel and store discounts. Some hotels and resorts offer on-site living quarters, meals, and laundry services. Year-end bonuses up to 25 percent of their basic salary are sometimes awarded to managers, depending on the employer.

WORK ENVIRONMENT

Executive housekeepers should expect to be on their feet much of their workday. They must perform walk-arounds of the entire hotel property to inspect any areas that may not be up to par with hotel standards. They also spend time forecasting with other hotel executives, meeting with different suppliers and vendors, and ironing out problems with staff.

The hours are long and stressful. Many executive housekeepers work 10 or more hours a day in order to touch base with all three work shifts. Some weekend and holiday work can be expected, depending on the business demands.

OUTLOOK

The outlook for this occupation is mixed. According to the *2003 Lodging Industry Profile,* compiled by the American Hotel and Lodging Association, the lodging industry is rebounding and is expected to weather any slow periods in the near future. The tourism industry is currently the third largest retail industry in the United States, behind automobiles and food stores.

The *Occupational Outlook Handbook* reports that employment for all lodging managers—including executive housekeepers—will grow about as fast as the average over the next decade. Several key factors—among them more international business travel, rising personal incomes, continued growth of the two-income family, and increased emphasis on leisure time and travel—contribute to the need for hotels and qualified people to maintain them. Certification, education, and standardization efforts are helping to give this field the more professional image it deserves. Without the reputation of a clean house, no hotel has a chance for success.

FOR MORE INFORMATION

For information on the hotel industry, career opportunities, and scholarships, contact the following organizations:

American Hotel and Lodging Association
1201 New York Avenue, NW, Suite 600
Washington, DC 20005-3931
Tel: 202-289-3100
Email: info@ahla.com
http://www.ahma.com

For information on internships, scholarships, or certification requirements, contact

Educational Institute of the American Hotel and Lodging Association
800 North Magnolia Avenue, Suite 1800
Orlando, FL 32803
Tel: 407-999-8100
Email: info@ei-ahla.org
http://www.ei-ahla.org

For a list of school programs, contact

International Council on Hotel, Restaurant, and Institutional Education
2810 North Parham Road, Suite 203
Richmond, VA 23294
Tel: 804-346-4800
http://chrie.org

For information on certification, contact

International Executive Housekeepers Association
1001 Eastwind Drive, Suite 301
Westerville, OH 43081-3361
Tel: 800-200-6342
http://www.ieha.org

Hotel Restaurant Managers

OVERVIEW

Hotel restaurant managers oversee the operation of hotel restaurants. They recruit and train staff, keep inventory of food supplies, handle customer complaints, and prepare the menu. They may also supervise the activities of the hotel's main restaurant as well as the cocktail lounge, banquets, and any food ordered through room service. There are approximately 371,000 restaurant managers employed in the United States, many of whom work in hotel restaurants.

HISTORY

Early hotels and motels offered simple meals to their guests, often prepared and served by the innkeeper or members of the family. As lodging became more sophisticated and offered more amenities to attract guests, portions of the hotel were designated as areas to serve food—the hotel restaurant was born. Some owners found themselves trying to manage more departments of the hotel than they were capable, or in some cases, numerous lodging facilities. Owners then turned to trusted employees for managing specific areas of their hotel, one of which, oftentimes, was the hotel restaurant.

Ellsworth Statler, founder of the Statler Hotels, was a great supporter of the hotel restaurant. He set a standard of quality and service in lodging, and made his hotels available to middle America. Statler's hotels had clean, comfortable rooms with a private bath, telephone, and radio. Statler hotels also had restaurants with house recipes, linens, china, and silverware.

Restaurants were almost exclusively associated with hotels. It was common for the public, as well as hotel patrons, to enjoy a cocktail with dinner at the hotel restaurant or have a drink at the hotel bar. The 1920s and the start of Prohibition, however, brought the Volstead Act that outlawed the consumption of any alcohol in the United States. People then turned to speakeasies, facilities that served alcohol illegally. In time, speakeasies offered food to their customers. Prohibition thus helped drive a wedge between the hotel and the restaurant, two institutions that traditionally had coexisted for mutual profit.

Today, most hotels offer some type of food service. Many have room service available for hotel patrons, and restaurants, pubs, cocktail lounges, and cafeterias open to the public. The position of restaurant manager has proven essential for the successful operation of hotel food and beverage service.

THE JOB

The efficient and profitable management of a hotel restaurant falls on the shoulders of its restaurant manager. In a hotel or motel, the restaurant manager oversees the many duties involving food service—the restaurants or cafes housed inside the hotel, the cocktail lounges, and, sometimes, the room service department. In larger hotels and motels, the restaurant manager may receive help from one or more assistant managers and executive chefs. *Assistant restaurant managers* supervise the dining rooms and other areas of food management, as needed. *Executive chefs* oversee operations in the kitchen, from food preparation to final presentation. *Bookkeepers* are sometimes hired to help with administrative details. Assistant managers, executive chefs, and bookkeepers report to the restaurant manager. However, especially in smaller lodging establishments, the restaurant manager is expected to perform with very little support.

A very important duty of the restaurant manager is the ordering and receiving of supplies. On a daily basis, the restaurant manager must check and monitor food consumption, and then place orders with different vendors as needed. Perishables, such as fresh fruits, vegetables, and meats, need to be ordered many times during the week. Deliveries need to consistently meet the hotel's standard of quality. Supplies of linens, tableware, cooking and serving utensils, and cleaning supplies as well as larger items, such as furniture and fixtures, are kept in order by the manager.

No food establishment would succeed without competent, hardworking servers, cooks, dining room attendants, and hosts. Interviewing, hiring, training, and even firing these workers are also the responsibility of the restaurant manager. Weekly work schedules are made to ensure coverage during peak dining times, while giving all employees equal and fair hours of work.

Administrative work is another primary obligation of the restaurant manager. Accurate hourly work records, wages, and taxes are some examples of paperwork needed to prepare payrolls. Managers must also keep tallies of supplies and equipment ordered and received. Computers have eased the workload tremendously in the past few years. Software such as point-of-service (POS) systems allow for restaurants to keep track of employee productivity as well as sale progress of menu items. Using a POS system, the waiter or waitress inputs the diner's menu order and it is immediately sent to the kitchen for preparation. The same information is used by the computer to total food and beverage orders into the final check. If the customer is paying with a credit card, a POS system can immediately verify the card number. Many managers use a POS system's daily tallies of food and drinks ordered to keep inventory supplies well stocked and current. Sometimes, additional supplies are ordered from specific vendors using this system.

Supervision of the dining rooms and kitchen is not as simple as it sounds. Food must be prepared, presented, and served correctly—in a timely manner. The kitchen staff must meet government regulations on sanitary standards of food preparation. Managers may meet with the chef regularly to analyze recipes for ingredients, portion size, labor, and overhead costs in order to assign a menu price. Menus need to be updated from time to time, and additional supplies must be ordered ahead of time for new menu items.

Not all duties of the restaurant manager are exciting or pleasant. They also receive and professionally resolve customer complaints, even if the criticisms come at the busiest and most inopportune times. Managers must be versatile enough to be able to pitch in where help is needed most: seating guests, serving food, clearing tables, or taking food orders. Restaurant managers are among the first to arrive at the hotel restaurant and most often do not leave until all sales receipts are tallied, equipment is shut down, lights are dimmed, and alarm systems are started.

REQUIREMENTS

High School
The food and beverage department is one of the best places to start in the hotel industry since there are so many positions to fill. Many

entry-level food service jobs may lead to better-paying and more responsible positions if the worker shows enough drive and potential.

You can prepare for a career in hotel restaurant management by taking a wide range of classes, especially business, English, and communication courses. Home economics classes would also be helpful. Vince Vito is a food and beverage manager for Hyatt Hotels in Oak Brook, Illinois. He found his high school marketing and business administration classes helpful in preparing for this career.

Postsecondary Training

People interested in restaurant management usually study business administration combined with food service or home economics in college. Some classes to consider are marketing, business systems, nutrition, and food preparation. As always, it pays to have the advantage of work experience to back up a solid education. Part-time or seasonal work in a hotel's food service department during college will be a definite foot in the door come interview time.

Certification or Licensing

Certification in the hotel food service industry is not mandatory, but it is definitely a recognized and respected achievement. The Education Institute of the American Hotel and Lodging Association, among other institutions, offers certification programs to all levels of hotel employment, from entry-level positions to upper management. Many hotels use levels of certification as a pay-scale guide. The National Restaurant Association offers the foodservice management professional credential to restaurant mangers who meet experience and training requirements.

High school juniors and seniors who are interested in working in the hospitality industry can take advantage of the *Educational Institute of the American Hotel and Lodging Association's Lodging* Management Program. The program combines classroom learning with work experience in the hospitality industry. Graduating seniors who pass examinations and work in the lodging industry for at least 30 days receive the certified rooms division specialist designation. Visit http://www.lodgingmanagement.org for more information.

Other Requirements

This is a demanding industry. Being a hotel restaurant manager can be taxing, both physically and mentally. Can you deal with many different types of people in various situations? Be a team player yet stay a successful and effective supervisor? Brush up on your communication skills; you'll definitely need them for this job.

EXPLORING

Many hotels and motels are willing to hire students like yourself to work banquets, as waiters, waitresses, dining room attendants, or inside the kitchen. This would provide work experience in the field of food service as well as a way to earn good spending money.

Vince Vito had the foresight to begin part-time hotel work while a senior in high school. His job title was bellman, but he was not limited to carrying luggage. "I was working all over the hotel—from the banquet room, to the front desk, to getting toothbrushes for hotel guests," Vito says. He recommends that high school students find hotel work in any capacity, just to get valuable experience.

EMPLOYERS

Hotels located in large urban areas, or those near the airport, most often house restaurants. Also, many hotels have cocktail lounges, pubs, banquet facilities, room service, and counter-type eateries that need capable people to manage them. A top name in the industry is Marriott International, which gives additional training and support to women and minority employees on the management track.

STARTING OUT

Job openings are posted at job fairs, in hotel trade magazines, and in newspapers. National organizations are also great sources of information for jobs. Check with the National Restaurant Association or the American Hotel and Lodging Association for information, or better yet, log on to their websites for job descriptions and openings nationwide. Don't forget to use the resources any regional or state lodging association may have to offer (look in the phone book for associations in your area).

Use any contacts you made during part-time work or on your internships. Networking is a helpful strategy when job hunting. Let everyone know you are ready for full-time employment.

ADVANCEMENT

Many restaurant managers move to management services—food services provided by hotels for business cafeterias, banks, and schools. Another area for advancement is into industrial food service, hotel food and beverage departments that work with health care or assisted-living institutions. The industrial side is not necessarily more lucrative, but the hours are more stable. Managers usually work nine to five and have their weekends and holidays off unless special projects or events are planned. Another advancement possibility is into the job of *restaurant director*. This person supervises the overall management of food service within the hotel. Restaurant managers report to the restaurant director.

Many experienced hotel restaurant managers are promoted to the executive side of hotel management. Having the responsibility of running a business that contributes large revenues to the hotel makes restaurant managers good candidates for higher rungs on the corporate ladder.

EARNINGS

According to the U.S. Department of Labor, all food service managers earned a median salary of $39,610 in 2004. The lowest 10 percent earned less than $24,500 and the highest 10 percent earned more than $68,860. Those working in hotels and motels earned higher salaries than most managers, with a median annual salary of $43,660.

Benefit packages include vacation and sick time, health, and sometimes dental, insurance, savings plans as well as 401(k) or pension plans. Some companies offer bonus incentives and discounted employee rates for lodging and food.

WORK ENVIRONMENT

Hotel restaurants have long hours—some are open 24 hours a day. It's not uncommon for restaurant managers to work 50 to 60 hours a week. Expect late hours if closing the restaurant, or early hours if opening one for breakfast. Managers are the backbone of a successful eatery, so many times they are called on to work weekends and holidays. It would be safe to say their lives revolve around the restaurant, the hotel, and the demands of business.

The key to success is to remain calm and levelheaded no matter how tough the day, how uncooperative the employee, or how irate the customer. Roberta Jackson, manager for Allie's, a Marriott hotel restaurant, advises, "Don't ever prejudge a situation; keep yourself open. That way you can learn many things to enhance yourself for the next day."

OUTLOOK

According to the *Occupational Outlook Handbook,* employment for food service managers is expected to grow about as fast as the average for all occupations through 2012. Job prospects for managers of hotel restaurants should be particularly good, as the amount of business and leisure travel continues to increase. Managers working for larger national chains and franchises such as Hyatt Hotels or Marriott International are better protected by the hotel's reputation than self-employed managers or those working for single-standing operations.

FOR MORE INFORMATION

For information on the hotel industry, career opportunities, and scholarships, contact the following organizations:
American Hotel and Lodging Association
1201 New York Avenue, NW, Suite 600
Washington, DC 20005-3931
Tel: 202-289-3100
Email: info@ahla.com
http://www.ahma.com

For information on certification, contact
Educational Institute of the American Hotel and Lodging Association
800 North Magnolia Avenue, Suite 1800
Orlando, FL 32803
Tel: 407-999-8100
Email: info@ei-ahla.org
http://www.ei-ahla.org

For information on educational programs and scholarships, contact
International Council on Hotel, Restaurant and Institutional Education
2810 North Parham Road, Suite 203
Richmond, VA 23294
Tel: 804-346-4800
http://chrie.org

For information on certification, careers, high school hospitality courses, and financial aid, contact
National Restaurant Association Educational Foundation
175 West Jackson Boulevard, Suite 1500
Chicago, IL 60604-2814
Tel: 800-765-2122
http://www.nraef.org or http://www.restaurant.org/careers

Interpreters and Translators

OVERVIEW

An *interpreter* translates spoken passages of a foreign language into another specified language. The job is often designated by the language interpreted, such as Spanish or Japanese. In addition, many interpreters specialize according to subject matter. For example, *medical interpreters* have extensive knowledge of and experience in the health care field, while *court or judiciary interpreters* speak both a second language and the "language" of law. *Interpreters for the deaf,* also known as *sign language interpreters,* aid in the communication between people who are unable to hear and those who can.

In contrast to interpreters, *translators* focus on written materials, such as books, plays, technical or scientific papers, legal documents, laws, treaties, and decrees. A *sight translator* performs a combination of interpreting and translating by reading printed material in one language while reciting it aloud in another.

There are approximately 31,000 interpreters and translators employed in the United States.

HISTORY

Until recently, most people who spoke two languages well enough to interpret and translate did so only on the side, working full time in some other occupation. For example, many diplomats and high-level government officials employed people who were able to serve as interpreters and translators, but only as needed. These employees spent the rest of their time assisting in other ways.

Interpreting and translating as full-time professions have emerged only recently, partly in response to the need for high-speed communication across the globe. The increasing use of complex diplomacy has also increased demand for full-time translating and interpreting professionals. For many years, diplomacy was practiced largely between just two nations. Rarely did conferences involve more than two languages at one time. The League of Nations, established by the Treaty of Versailles in 1919, established a new pattern of communication. Although the "language of diplomacy" was then considered to be French, diplomatic discussions were carried out in many different languages for the first time.

Since the early 1920s, multinational conferences have become commonplace. Trade and educational conferences are now held with participants of many nations in attendance. Responsible for international diplomacy after the League of Nations dissolved, the United Nations (UN) now employs many full-time interpreters and translators, providing career opportunities for qualified people. In addition, the European Union employs a large number of interpreters.

THE JOB

Although interpreters are needed for a variety of languages and different venues and circumstances, there are only two basic systems of interpretation: simultaneous and consecutive. Spurred in part by the invention and development of electronic sound equipment, simultaneous interpretation has been in use since the charter of the UN.

Simultaneous interpreters are able to convert a spoken sentence instantaneously. Some are so skilled that they are able to complete a sentence in the second language at almost the precise moment that the speaker is conversing in the original language. Such interpreters are usually familiar with the speaking habits of the speaker and can anticipate the way in which the sentence will be completed. The interpreter may also make judgments about the intent of the sentence or phrase from the speaker's gestures, facial expressions, and inflections. While working at a fast pace, the interpreter must be careful not to summarize, edit, or in any way change the meaning of what is being said.

In contrast, *consecutive interpreters* wait until the speaker has paused to convert speech into a second language. In this case, the speaker waits until the interpreter has finished before resuming the speech. Since every sentence is repeated in consecutive interpretation, this method takes longer than simultaneous interpretation.

Profile: Maximilian Berlitz

Maximilian D. Berlitz emigrated from Germany to the United States in 1872. After enjoying a successful career as a private language instructor (in Greek, Latin, and six other European languages), Berlitz became a professor of French and German at the Warner Polytechnic College in Providence, Rhode Island, where at one time he served as the institution's owner, dean, principal, and only professor.

Overworked and in need of an assistant to teach French, Berlitz hired Nicholas Joly—only to later discover that Joly did not speak English. Trying to find a way to both communicate with the Frenchman and use him at the college, Berlitz indicated that Joly should point to objects and act out verbs, while at the same time, naming them in French.

The result? Students began participating in dynamic question-and-answer sessions with Joly—all in elegant French! The formality of the classroom had disappeared. In its place, Berlitz found that he had quite accidentally developed an innovative teaching technique that kept students alert and interested. Today, people can go to over 300 Berlitz centers around the world in order to learn languages needed for business or personal travel.

In both systems, interpreters are placed so that they can clearly see and hear all that is taking place. In formal situations, such as those at the UN and other international conferences, interpreters are often assigned to a glass-enclosed booth. Speeches are transmitted to the booth, and interpreters, in turn, translate the speaker's words into a microphone. Each UN delegate can tune in the voice of the appropriate interpreter. Because of the difficulty of the job, these simultaneous interpreters usually work in pairs, each working 30-minute shifts.

All international *conference interpreters* are simultaneous interpreters. Many interpreters, however, work in situations other than formal diplomatic meetings. For example, interpreters are needed for negotiations of all kinds, as well as for legal, financial, medical, and business purposes. *Court or judiciary interpreters*, for example, work in courtrooms and at attorney-client meetings, depositions, and witness preparation sessions.

Other interpreters known as *guide or escort interpreters* serve on call, traveling with visitors from foreign countries who are touring the United States. Usually, these language specialists use consecutive interpretation. Their job is to make sure that whatever the visitors say is understood and that they also understand what is being said to them. Still other interpreters accompany groups of U.S. citizens on official tours abroad. On such assignments, they may be sent to any foreign country and might be away from the United States for long periods of time.

Interpreters also work on short-term assignments. Services may be required for only brief intervals, such as for a special conference or single interview with press representatives.

While interpreters focus on the spoken word, translators work with written language. They read and translate novels, plays, essays, nonfiction and technical works, legal documents, records and reports, speeches, and other written material. Translators generally follow a certain set of procedures in their work. They begin by reading the text, taking careful notes on what they do not understand. To translate questionable passages, they look up words and terms in specialized dictionaries and glossaries. They may also do additional reading on the subject to arrive at a better understanding. Finally, they write translated drafts in the target language.

Localization translation is a relatively new specialty. *Localization translators* adapt computer software, websites, and other business products for use in a different language or culture.

REQUIREMENTS
High School
If you are interested in becoming an interpreter or translator, you should take a variety of English courses, because most translating work is from a foreign language into English. The study of one or more foreign languages is vital. If you are interested in becoming proficient in one or more of the Romance languages, such as Italian, French, or Spanish, basic courses in Latin will be valuable.

While you should devote as much time as possible to the study of at least one foreign language, other helpful courses include speech, business, cultural studies, humanities, world history, geography, and political science. In fact, any course that emphasizes the written and/or spoken word will be valuable to aspiring interpreters or translators. In addition, knowledge of a particular subject matter in which you may have interest, such as health, law, or science, will give you a professional edge if you want to specialize. Finally, courses in typing and word processing are recommended, especially if you want to pursue a career as a translator.

Postsecondary Training
Because interpreters and translators need to be proficient in grammar, have an excellent vocabulary in the chosen language, and have

sound knowledge in a wide variety of subjects, employers generally require that applicants have at least a bachelor's degree. Scientific and professional interpreters are best qualified if they have graduate degrees.

In addition to language and field-specialty skills, you should take college courses that will allow you to develop effective techniques in public speaking, particularly if you're planning to pursue a career as an interpreter. Courses such as speech and debate will improve your diction and confidence as a public speaker.

Hundreds of colleges and universities in the United States offer degrees in languages. In addition, educational institutions now provide programs and degrees specialized for interpreting and translating. Georgetown University (http://www.georgetown.edu/departments/linguistics) offers both undergraduate and graduate programs in linguistics. The Translation Studies Program at the University of Texas at Brownsville (http://www.utb.edu) allows students to earn certificates in translation studies at the undergraduate level. Graduate degrees in interpretation and translation may be earned at the University of California at Santa Barbara (http://www.ucsb.edu), the University of Puerto Rico (http://www.upr.clu.edu), and the Monterey Institute of International Studies (http://www.miis.edu/languages.html). Many of these programs include both general and specialized courses, such as medical interpretation and legal translation.

Academic programs for the training of interpreters can be found in Europe as well. The University of Geneva's School of Translation and Interpretation (http://www.unige.ch/eti/en) is highly regarded among professionals in the field.

Certification or Licensing

Although interpreters and translators need not be certified to obtain jobs, employers often show preference to certified applicants. Certification in Spanish, Haitian, Creole, and Navajo is also required for interpreters who are employed by federal courts. State and local courts often have their own specific certification requirements. The National Center for State Courts has more information on certification for these workers. Interpreters for the deaf who pass an examination may qualify for either comprehensive or legal certification by the Registry of Interpreters for the Deaf.

The U.S. Department of State has a three-test requirement for interpreters. These include simple consecutive interpreting (escort), simultaneous interpreting (court/seminar), and conference-level interpreting (international conferences). Applicants must have several years of foreign language practice, advanced education in the language (preferably abroad), and be fluent in vocabulary for a very broad range of subjects.

Foreign language translators may be granted certification by the American Translators Association (ATA) upon successful completion of required exams. ATA certification is available for translators who translate the following languages into English: Arabic, Danish, Dutch, French, German, Hungarian, Italian, Japanese, Polish, Portuguese, Russian, and Spanish. Certification is also available for translators who translate English into the following languages: Chinese, Dutch, Finnish, French, German, Hungarian, Italian, Japanese, Polish, Portuguese, Russian, and Spanish.

Other Requirements

Interpreters should be able to speak at least two languages fluently, without strong accents. They should be knowledgeable of not only the foreign language but also of the culture and social norms of the region or country in which it is spoken. Both interpreters and translators should read daily newspapers in the languages in which they work to keep current in both developments and usage.

Interpreters must have good hearing, a sharp mind, and a strong, clear, and pleasant voice. They must be able to be precise and quick in their translation. In addition to being flexible and versatile in their work, both interpreters and translators should have self-discipline and patience. Above all, they should have an interest in and love of language.

Finally, interpreters must be honest and trustworthy, observing any existing codes of confidentiality at all times. The ethical code of interpreters and translators is a rigid one. They must hold private proceedings in strict confidence. Ethics also demands that interpreters and translators not distort the meaning of the sentences that are spoken or written. No matter how much they may agree or disagree with the speaker or writer, interpreters and translators must be objective in their work. In addition, information they obtain in the process of interpretation or translation must never be passed along to unauthorized people or groups.

EXPLORING

If you have an opportunity to visit the United Nations, you can watch the proceedings to get some idea of the techniques and responsibilities of the job of the interpreter. Occasionally, an international conference session is televised, and the work of the interpreters can be observed. You should note, however, that interpreters who work at these conferences are in the top positions of the vocation. Not everyone may aspire to such jobs. The work of interpreters and translators is usually less public, but not necessarily less interesting.

If you have adequate skills in a foreign language, you might consider traveling in a country in which the language is spoken. If you can converse easily and without a strong accent and can interpret to others who may not understand the language well, you may have what it takes to work as an interpreter or translator.

For any international field, it is important that you familiarize yourself with other cultures. You can even arrange to regularly correspond with a pen pal in a foreign country. You may also want to join a school club that focuses on a particular language, such as the French Club or the Spanish Club. If no such clubs exist, consider forming one. Student clubs can allow you to hone your foreign language speaking and writing skills and learn about other cultures.

Finally, participating on a speech or debate team can allow you to practice your public speaking skills, increase your confidence, and polish your overall appearance by working on eye contact, gestures, facial expressions, tone, and other elements used in public speaking.

EMPLOYERS

There are approximately 31,000 interpreters and translators in the United States. Although many interpreters and translators work for government or international agencies, some are employed by private firms. Large import-export companies often have interpreters or translators on their payrolls, although these employees generally perform additional duties for the firm. International banks, companies, organizations, and associations often employ both interpreters and translators to facilitate communication. In addition, translators and interpreters work at publishing houses, schools, bilingual newspapers, radio and television stations, airlines, shipping companies, law firms, and scientific and medical operations.

While translators are employed nationwide, a large number of interpreters find work in New York and Washington, D.C. Among the largest employers of interpreters and translators are the United Nations, the World Bank, the U.S. Department of State, the Bureau of the Census, the CIA, the FBI, the Library of Congress, the Red Cross, the YMCA, and the armed forces.

Approximately 4,600 interpreters and translators work independently in private practice. These self-employed professionals must be disciplined and driven, since they must handle all aspects of the business such as scheduling work and billing clients.

STARTING OUT

Most interpreters and translators begin as part-time freelancers until they gain experience and contacts in the field. Individuals can apply for jobs directly to the hiring firm, agency, or organization. Many of these employers advertise available positions in the classified section of the newspaper or on the Internet. In addition, contact your college placement office and language department to inquire about job leads.

While many opportunities exist, top interpreting and translating jobs are hard to obtain since the competition for these higher profile positions is fierce. You may be wise to develop supplemental skills that can be attractive to employers while refining your interpreting and translating techniques. The UN, for example, employs administrative assistants who can take shorthand and transcribe notes in two or more languages. The UN also hires tour guides who speak more than one language. Such positions can be initial steps toward your future career goals.

ADVANCEMENT

Competency in language determines the speed of advancement for interpreters and translators. Job opportunities and promotions are plentiful for those who have acquired great proficiency in languages. However, interpreters and translators need to constantly work and study to keep abreast of the changing linguistic trends for a given language. The constant addition of new vocabulary for technological advances, inventions, and processes keep languages fluid. Those who do not keep up with changes will find that their communication skills become quickly outdated.

Interpreters and translators who work for government agencies advance by clearly defined grade promotions. Those who work for other organizations can aspire to become chief interpreters or chief translators, or *reviewers* who check the work of others.

Although advancement in the field is generally slow, interpreters and translators will find many opportunities to succeed as freelancers. Some can even establish their own bureaus or agencies.

EARNINGS

Earnings for interpreters and translators vary, depending on experience, skills, number of languages used, and employers. According to the U.S. Department of Labor, interpreters and translators earned a median hourly wage of $16.28 in 2004 (about $33,860 a year).

Wages ranged from less than $9.67 an hour ($20,130 a year) to more than $27.45 an hour ($57,000 a year).

Interpreters who are employed by the United Nations work under a salary structure called the Common System. In 2003, UN short-term interpreters (workers employed for a duration of 60 days or less) had daily gross pay of $447.50 (Grade I) or $291.50 (Grade II). UN short-term translators and revisers had daily gross pay of $186.75 (Translator I), $230.50 (Translator II), $275.45 (Translator III/Reviser I), $312.80 (Translator IV/Reviser II), or $350.15 (Reviser III).

Depending on the employer, interpreters and translators often enjoy such benefits as health and life insurance, pension plans, and paid vacation and sick days.

WORK ENVIRONMENT

Interpreters and translators work under a wide variety of circumstances and conditions. As a result, most do not have typical nine-to-five schedules.

Conference interpreters probably have the most comfortable physical facilities in which to work. Their glass-enclosed booths are well lit and temperature controlled. Court or judiciary interpreters work in courtrooms or conference rooms, while interpreters for the deaf work at educational institutions as well as a wide variety of other locations.

Interpreters who work for escort or tour services are often required to travel for long periods of time. Their schedules are dictated by the group or person for whom they are interpreting. A freelance interpreter may work out of one city or be assigned anywhere in the world as needed.

Translators usually work in offices, although many spend considerable time in libraries and research centers. Freelance translators often work at home, using their own personal computers, the Internet, dictionaries, and other resource materials.

While both interpreting and translating require flexibility and versatility, interpreters in particular, especially those who work for international congresses or courts, may experience considerable stress and fatigue. Knowing that a great deal depends upon their absolute accuracy in interpretation can be a weighty responsibility.

OUTLOOK

Employment opportunities for interpreters and translators are expected to grow faster than the average through 2014, according to the U.S. Department of Labor. However, competition for available positions will be fierce. Opportunities should be best for interpreters and translators of the languages referred to as PFIGS (Portuguese, French, Italian, German, and Spanish) and the principal Asian languages of Chinese, Japanese, and Korean.

With the explosion of such technologies as the Internet, lightning-fast Internet connections, and videoconferencing, global communication has taken great strides. In short, the world has become smaller, so to speak, creating a demand for professionals to aid in the communication between people of different languages and cultural backgrounds.

In addition to new technological advances, demographic factors will fuel demand for translators and interpreters. Although some immigrants who come to the United States assimilate easily with respect to culture and language, many have difficulty learning English. As immigration to the United States continues to increase, interpreters and translators will be needed to help immigrants function in an English-speaking society. According to Ann Macfarlane, past president of the American Translators Association, "community interpreting" for immigrants and refugees is a challenging area requiring qualified language professionals.

Another demographic factor influencing the interpreting and translating fields is the growth in overseas travel. Americans on average are spending an increasing amount of money on travel, especially to foreign countries. The resulting growth of the travel industry will create a need for interpreters to lead tours, both at home and abroad.

In addition to leisure travel, business travel is spurring the need for more translators and interpreters. With workers traveling abroad in growing numbers to attend meetings, conferences, and seminars with overseas clients, interpreters and translators will be needed to help bridge both the language and cultural gaps.

While no more than a few thousand interpreters and translators are employed in the largest markets (the federal government and international organizations), other job options exist. The medical field, for example, will provide many jobs for language professionals, translating such products as pharmaceutical inserts, research papers, and medical reports for insurance companies. Interpreters will also be needed to provide non-English speakers with language assistance in health care settings. Opportunities exist for qualified individuals in law, trade and business, health care, tourism, recreation, and the government.

FOR MORE INFORMATION

For more on the translating and interpreting professions, including information on accreditation, contact

American Translators Association
225 Reinekers Lane, Suite 590
Alexandria, VA 22314
Tel: 703-683-6100
Email: ata@atanet.org
http://www.atanet.org

For more information on court interpreting and certification, contact

National Association of Judiciary Interpreters and Translators
603 Stewart St., Suite 610
Seattle, WA 98101
Tel: 206-267-2300
Email: headquarters@najit.org
http://www.najit.org

For information on interpreter training programs for working with the deaf and certification, contact

Registry of Interpreters for the Deaf
333 Commerce Street
Alexandria, VA 22314
Tel: 703-838-0030
TTY: 703-838-0459
Email: membership@rid.org
http://www.rid.org

For information on union membership for freelance interpreters and translators, contact

Translators and Interpreters Guild
962 Wayne Avenue, #500
Silver Spring, MD 20910
Tel: 800-992-0367
Email: info@ttig.org
http://www.ttig.org

Reservation and Ticket Agents

OVERVIEW

Reservation and ticket agents are employed by airlines, bus companies, railroads, and cruise lines to help customers in several ways. *Reservation agents* make and confirm travel arrangements for passengers by using computers and manuals to determine timetables, taxes, and other information.

Ticket agents sell tickets in terminals or in separate offices. Like reservation agents, they also use computers and manuals containing scheduling, boarding, and rate information to plan routes and calculate ticket costs. They determine whether seating is available, answer customer inquiries, check baggage, and direct passengers to proper places for boarding. They may also announce arrivals and departures and assist passengers in boarding. There are approximately 163,000 reservation and ticket agents employed in the United States.

HISTORY

Since the earliest days of commercial passenger transportation (by boat or stagecoach), someone has been responsible for making sure that space is available and that everyone on board pays the proper fare. As transportation grew into a major industry over the years, the job of making reservations and selling tickets became a specialized occupation.

The airline industry experienced its first boom in the early 1930s. By the end of that decade, millions of people were flying each year. Since

QUICK FACTS

School Subjects
Business
Computer science
English

Personal Skills
Communication/ideas
Helping/teaching

Work Environment
Primarily indoors
Primarily one location

Minimum Education Level
Some postsecondary training

Salary Range
$17,720 to $27,750 to
$45,100

Certification or Licensing
None available

Outlook
More slowly than the
average

DOT
238

GOE
11.03.01

NOC
6433

O*NET-SOC
43-4181.00, 43-4181.01,
43-4181.02

the introduction of passenger-carrying jet planes in 1958, the number of people traveling by air has multiplied many times over. Airlines now employ about six out of every 10 reservation and ticket agents.

A number of innovations have helped make the work of reservation and ticket agents easier and more efficient. The introduction of automated telephone services allows customers to check on flight availability and arrival/departure times without having to wait to speak to an agent. Computers have both simplified the agents' work and put more resources within their reach. Since the 1950s, many airlines have operated computerized scheduling and reservation systems, either individually or in partnership with other airlines. Until recently, these systems were not available to the general consumer. In the last decade, however, the growth of the Internet has permitted travelers to access scheduling and rate information, make reservations, and purchase tickets without contacting an agent. Airlines now offer electronic tickets, which they expect will eventually replace the traditional paper ticket. Despite these innovations, there will always be a need for reservation and ticketing agents, primarily for safety and security purposes. These employees still fill a vital role in the transportation industry.

THE JOB

Airline reservation agents are sales agents who work in large central offices run by airline companies. Their primary job is to book and confirm reservations for passengers on scheduled flights. At the request of the customer or a ticket agent, they plan the itinerary and other travel arrangements. While many agents still use timetables, airline manuals, reference guides, and tariff books, most of this work is performed using specialized computer programs.

Computers are used to make, confirm, change, and cancel reservations. After asking for the passenger's destination, desired travel time, and airport of departure, reservation agents type the information into a computer and quickly obtain information on all flight schedules and seating availability. If the plane is full, the agent may suggest an alternative flight or check to see if space is available on another airline that flies to the same destination. Agents may even book seats on competing airlines, especially if their own airline can provide service on the return trip.

Reservation agents also answer telephone inquiries about such things as schedules, fares, arrival and departure times, and cities serviced by their airline. They may maintain an inventory of passenger space available so they can notify other personnel and ticket stations

Reservation and ticket agents must be able to answer passengers' questions correctly, quickly, and courteously. *(Getty Images)*

of changes and try to book all flights to capacity. Some reservation agents work in more specialized areas, handling calls from travel agents or booking flights for members of frequent flyer programs. Agents working with international airlines must also be informed of visa regulations and other travel developments. This information is usually supplied by the *senior reservation agent,* who supervises and coordinates the activities of the other agents.

In the railroad industry, *train reservation clerks* perform similar tasks. They book seats or compartments for passengers, keep station agents and clerks advised on available space, and communicate with reservation clerks in other towns.

General transportation ticket agents for any mode of travel (air, bus, rail, or ship) sell tickets to customers at terminals or at separate ticket offices. Like reservation agents, they book space for customers. In addition, they use computers to prepare and print tickets, calculate fares, and collect payment. At the terminals they check and tag luggage, direct passengers to the proper areas for boarding, keep records of passengers on each departure, and help with customer problems, such as lost baggage or missed connections. Airline ticket agents may have additional duties, such as paging arriving and departing passengers and finding accommodations or new travel arrangements for passengers in the event of flight cancellations.

In airports, *gate agents* assign seats, issue boarding passes, make public address announcements of departures and arrivals, and help elderly or disabled passengers board the planes. In addition, they may also provide information to disembarking passengers about ground transportation, connecting flights, and local hotels.

Regardless of where they work, reservation and transportation ticket agents must be knowledgeable about their companies' policies and procedures, as well as the standard procedures of their industry. They must be aware of the availability of special promotions and services and be able to answer any questions customers may have.

REQUIREMENTS

High School

Reservation and ticket agents are generally required to have at least a high school diploma. Applicants should be able to type and have good communication and problem-solving skills. Because computers are being used more and more in this field, you should have a basic knowledge of computers and computer software. Previous experience working with the public is also helpful for the job. Knowledge of geography and foreign languages are other valuable skills, especially for international service agents.

Postsecondary Training

Some college is preferred, although it is not considered essential for the job. Some colleges now offer courses specifically designed for ticket reservations.

Reservation agents are given about a month of classroom instruction. Here you will be taught how to read schedules, calculate fares, and plan itineraries. They learn how to use computer programs to get information and reserve space efficiently. They also study company policies and government regulations that apply to the industry.

Transportation ticket agents receive less training, consisting of about one week of classroom instruction. They learn how to read tickets and schedules, assign seats, and tag baggage. This is followed by one week of on-the-job training, working alongside an experienced agent. After mastering the simpler tasks, the new ticket agents are trained to reserve space, make out tickets, and handle the boarding gate.

Other Requirements

Because you will be in constant contact with the public, professional appearance, a clear and pleasant speaking voice, and a friendly personality are important qualities. You need to be tactful in keeping telephone time to a minimum without alienating your customers. In addition, you should enjoy working with people, have a good memory, and be able to maintain your composure when working with harried or unhappy travelers. Agents form a large part of the public image of their company.

Although not a requirement, many agents belong to labor unions such as the Transport Workers Union of America and the International Brotherhood of Teamsters.

EXPLORING

You may wish to apply for part-time or summer work with transportation companies in their central offices or at terminals. A school counselor can help you arrange an information interview with an experienced reservation and transportation ticket agent. Talking to an agent directly about his or her duties can help you to become more familiar with transportation operations.

EMPLOYERS

Reservation and ticket agents hold approximately 163,000 jobs in the United States. Commercial airlines are the main employers. However, other transportation companies, such as rail, ship, and bus lines, also require their services.

STARTING OUT

To find part-time or summer work, apply directly to the personnel or employment offices of transportation companies. Ask your school counselor or college placement director for information about job openings, requirements, and possible training programs. Additionally, contact transportation unions for lists of job openings.

ADVANCEMENT

With experience and a good work record, some reservation and ticket agents can be promoted to supervisory positions. They can also become city and district sales managers for ticket offices. Beyond this, opportunities for advancement are limited. However, achieving seniority within a company can give an agent the first choice of shifts and available overtime.

EARNINGS

According to the U.S. Department of Labor, reservation and transportation ticket agents earned median salaries of approximately $27,750 in 2004. The lowest paid 10 percent of these workers made less than $17,720 per year, while the highest paid 10 percent earned more than $45,100 annually.

Most agents can earn overtime pay; many employers also pay extra for night work. Benefits vary according to the place of work, experience, and union membership; however, most receive vacation and sick pay, health insurance, and retirement plans. Agents, especially those employed by the airlines, often receive free or reduced-fare transportation for themselves and their families.

WORK ENVIRONMENT

Reservation and ticket agents generally work 40 hours per week. Those working in reservations typically work in cubicles with their own computer terminals and telephone headsets. They are often on the telephone and behind their computers all day long. Conversations with customers and computer activity may be monitored and recorded by their supervisors for evaluation and quality reasons. Agents might also be required to achieve sales or reservations quotas. During holidays or when special promotions and discounts are being offered, agents are especially busy. At these times or during periods of severe weather, passengers may become difficult. Handling customer frustrations can be stressful, but agents must maintain composure and a pleasant manner when speaking with customers.

Ticket agents working in airports and train and bus stations face a busy and noisy environment. They may stand most of the day and lift heavy objects such as luggage and packages. During holidays and busy times, their work can become extremely hectic as they process long lines of waiting customers. Storms and other factors may delay or even cancel flights, trains, and bus services. Like reservation agents, ticket agents may be confronted with upset passengers, but must be able to maintain composure at all times.

OUTLOOK

According to the U.S. Department of Labor, employment for reservation and ticket agents is expected to grow more slowly than the average for all occupations through 2014. Technology is changing the way consumers purchase tickets. Ticketless travel and electronic ticketing—automated reservations ticketing—is reducing the need for agents. In addition, many airports now have computerized kiosks that allow passengers to reserve and purchase tickets themselves. Passengers can also access information about fares and flight times on the Internet, where they can also make reservations and purchase tickets. However, for security reasons, all of these services cannot be fully automated, so the need for reservation and transportation ticket agents will never be completely eliminated.

Most openings will occur as experienced agents transfer to other occupations or retire. Competition for jobs is fierce due to declining demand, low turnover, and because of the glamour and attractive travel benefits associated with the industry.

FOR MORE INFORMATION

For information on the airline industry, contact the FAA.
Federal Aviation Administration (FAA)
800 Independence Avenue, SW, Room 810
Washington, DC 20591
Tel: 202-366-4000
http://www.faa.gov

For statistics on international travel and tourism, visit the following website:
World Tourism Organization
Capitán Haya 42
28020 Madrid, Spain
Email: omt@world-tourism.org
http://www.world-tourism.org

Ski Resort Workers

OVERVIEW

Ski resorts offer many different types of employment opportunities. Qualified *ski resort workers* are needed to supervise the activities on ski slopes, run operations at the lodge, provide instruction to skiers, and ensure the safety of resort patrons. There are numerous ski resorts located throughout the United States and the world. Jobs are plentiful, though the majority of them are seasonal, lasting from November to April. There are approximately 490 ski resorts in the United States.

HISTORY

Skiing developed primarily as a means to travel from one place to another. Northern Europeans were the first people to wear skis, which they fashioned from tree branches. Armies used skis to travel snowy mountain regions beginning in the Middle Ages through World War II.

Though people started skiing for pleasure in the 18th century, it was not until the invention of the motorized ski lift in the 1930s that skiing grew in popularity. After World War II, hundreds of resorts opened to accommodate this growing form of recreation. Resorts, offering skiing opportunities combined with comfortable accommodations and entertainment, provided people with a new vacation alternative. In the United States, large ski communities, such as Vail and Aspen in Colorado, developed as a result of the sport. Today, many of these towns' principle revenues stem from skiing and related activities.

School Subjects
Business
Mathematics
Speech

Personal Skills
Following instructions
Leadership/management

Work Environment
Indoors and outdoors
Primarily one location

Minimum Education Level
High school diploma (for most positions)

Salary Range
$17,000 to $33,970 to $60,000

Certification or Licensing
Required for certain positions

Outlook
About as fast as the average

DOT
379

GOE
04.03.03

NOC
0632, 5254, 6435, 6661

O*NET-SOC
33-9092.00

There are three types of skiing—Alpine, or downhill; Nordic, or cross country; and Freestyle, which incorporates acrobatic movements, stunts, and dance elements. Most resorts cater to the Alpine type of skiing. Other popular snow activities are snowboarding and sledding.

THE JOB

Ski resort workers run the gamut from entry level to highly skilled. Each is important for maintaining the order and operations of the resort community. One of the largest departments is ski lift operation. *Ski lift operators* make sure skiers have safe transport. There are several steps taken daily before a ski lift is opened to the public. First, ice, snow, or tree branches are cleared from the machinery and the loading and unloading platforms. Next, all machinery and parts are cleaned and safety checked. Finally, an experienced member of the lift staff conducts a trial run.

There are three main sections of the lift: bottom, middle terminal, and the top. Workers at all stations help passengers on or off the lift safely. They collect and punch lift tickets, adjust seats or the speed of the lift, and spot check for loose or dangling items that may catch on the lift's machinery. They answer any inquiries passengers may have about the run, or address general questions. They give directions and make sure skiers stay on the slopes and trails designated for their level of expertise—beginner, intermediate, and expert. Workers must sometimes reprimand unruly passengers.

Skiers who monitor the runs and surrounding areas are called the *ski patrol*. Considered the police of the mountains, they are specially trained ski experts responsible for preventing accidents and maintaining the safety standards of the resort. They mark off trails and courses that are not safe for the public. Patrol members also help injured skiers off the slopes and to proper first aid stations, or in extreme cases, to an ambulance. Ski patrol members should be versed in emergency medical techniques, such as CPR and first aid.

A *certified ski instructor* can teach everything from basic maneuvers to more advanced techniques. Ski instruction at a resort is generally free or offered for a small fee. Whether in group classes or private lessons, ski instructors teach students how to avoid injury by skiing safely and responsibly.

Before skiers head for the moguls, they need proper equipment. Working in the supply houses is an example of an entry-level position. *Ski technicians* assist skiers in getting the proper-sized boots, skis, and poles. They may answer questions regarding equipment and how it works.

Most ski resorts have chalets or lodges that offer skiers a place to rest and grab refreshments between runs. More often than not, these lodges serve as gathering places in the evenings for drinks and socialization. Some jobs at lodges include wait staff, housekeeping staff, gift shop or ski shop employees, resort managers, and human resources staff.

REQUIREMENTS

High School
Education requirements vary depending on the facility and type of work involved, though most resorts expect at least a high school diploma for their entry-level positions. High school courses that will be helpful include general business, mathematics, speech, and physical education. Learning a foreign language will also be helpful, since many foreign visitors vacation at American ski resorts.

Postsecondary Training
Many resorts prefer to hire college students as seasonal help. Management positions usually require a college degree. Some institutions, such as the University of Maine at Farmington, offer a combined program of a bachelor's degree with a certificate concentration in the ski industry. The university's ski industries certificate program offers training in the following concentrations: ski business management, professional ski coaching and ski teaching, and adaptive ski teaching. Qualified students can link their passion for the sport with a degree in business, economics, rehabilitation services, or general studies.

Certification and Licensing
Entry-level jobs such as clerks, wait staff, and ski lift operators do not require certification. However, you must be certified to qualify as a professional ski instructor. Professional Ski Instructors of America offers certification in three categories: Adaptive, Alpine, and Nordic. Certification consists of skill tests, further education, and on-the-job experience. Satisfactory completion of a national certification exam is also required. Ski instructors must be recertified every one to two years, depending on the region in which they teach.

Other Requirements
All employees, especially those who deal with customers, are a reflection of the resort for which they work. Different jobs call for

Altitude Sickness

While generally not a medical emergency, feeling sick or disoriented is common for many people who are first visiting a ski resort in an altitude that is higher than what they are used to. Symptoms of altitude sickness include headache, nausea, fatigue, diarrhea or constipation, difficulty sleeping, agitation, shortness of breath, rapid heartbeat, nasal congestion, and coughing. According to ski professionals in Breckenridge, Colorado, you can minimize these symptoms by taking it easy on the first day or two after you arrive at a ski resort, limiting alcohol, caffeine and salty foods, eating lightly, drinking plenty of water, and getting adequate sleep.

different qualities in a worker. Responsibility is key when working the ski lift, as well as tact when confronting troublesome skiers. Ski instructors need to be physically fit, as well as patient and understanding with their students. Ski patrol members must be able to react quickly in emergencies and have the foresight to spot potential trouble situations.

Workers who speak a second language will have an advantage. Many ski enthusiasts from South America travel to the United States for world class skiing, so workers who are fluent in Spanish or Portuguese will have good job prospects. Most positions can be altered to accommodate employees who are physically challenged. It is best to check with each resort to learn their policies and employee requirements.

EMPLOYERS

Approximately 39 states have ski resorts. States having the highest number of ski resorts include New York, Michigan, Wisconsin, Pennsylvania, California, Minnesota, Vermont, Maine, and New Hampshire. Colorado is the most popular skiing state, where many communities such as Vail, Aspen, and Telluride have grown around the industry.

Workers who are interested in year-round employment should look for resorts that cater to year-round business. The Aspen Ski Company, for example, has four mountain ski areas in operation during the winter months and three hotels that are open all year. Many employees work the slopes from November to April and the golf courses the rest of the year.

STARTING OUT

Many resorts actively recruit at college campuses and job fairs. Phone interviews and online applications are becoming more prevalent in this field. There are also websites that work as online employment services. Visit them to find job descriptions, salary expectations, and job benefits.

It would be wise to first compile a list of resorts or locations that interest you. Trade magazines, such as *Powder, the Skier's Magazine* (http://www.powdermag.com) or *SKI* (http://www.skimag.com), as well as your local library, are helpful resources. Apply for work at least two seasons ahead—that means start looking for winter work in the summer to be considered for choice positions.

ADVANCEMENT

Advancement is determined by a worker's experience, skill, level of education, and also their starting position. Ski lift operators can be promoted to department supervisors of that division, general supervisors, and finally management. Ski instructors may begin their careers by giving beginner's lessons or children's lessons and then advance to intermediate- or expert-level classes. Experienced instructors with good reputations may develop a following of students. They may also be promoted to department supervisor or management. Lodge employees may be promoted to positions with increased responsibilities such as shift supervisor or manager.

EARNINGS

Salaries for ski resort workers vary depending on the resort, the region where it is located, and the type of position the worker holds. For example, managers of ski lodges fall under the category of hotel and motel managers, who made median annual salaries of $33,970 a year in 2004, with some managers of larger hotels making more than $60,000 a year. Ski instructors, who fall under the general category of fitness and sports instructors, made between $17,000 and $55,000 in 2004, with median annual earnings of $25,460. Large, well-established resorts, especially those located in the mountain states and northeast, tend to pay higher hourly rates.

Most ski resort employees are given complimentary full or partial season ski passes. Some companies also provide their employees with housing at or near the resort. Full-time employees receive the standard benefits package including paid vacation and health insurance.

WORK ENVIRONMENT

Ski slopes open at around 8:00 A.M. and close at dusk; many resorts light some courses, to allow for night skiing. Ski lift operators, ski patrol, ski instructors, and other employees assigned to outdoor work prepare for the often blustery weather by wearing layers of clothes, waterproof coats, ski pants, boots, hats, and gloves. Some resorts supply their employees with uniform coats and accessories.

There are also indoor positions available for ski resort workers. Employees who enjoy a warm and comfortable workplace and still have great customer contact include lodge workers, gift shop employees, and ski technicians. Most ski resort employees work about 40 hours a week; ski instructors' schedules will vary depending on their class load. Since ski resorts are open seven days a week, employees with low seniority are expected to work weekends and holidays—the busiest times for most resorts.

OUTLOOK

Emphasis on physical health, interest in sport-related vacations, and growing household incomes point to a bright future for ski resorts and their employees. And weather may not always hamper this industry. Many resorts, using snowmaking devices to create a snow-covered run, can extend the season well into April.

Note, however, that the majority of jobs in this industry are seasonal. Many students use this opportunity to supplement their income during school vacations, as well as fuel their interest in the sport. Some resorts offer year-round employment by shifting their employees to other jobs off season. Golf course attendants, tour guides, and spa workers are some examples of summer jobs. Workers who are interested in working in the management side of the business should consider pursuing degrees in business management, rehabilitation services, or physical education.

The travel and tourism industry is affected by the state of our nation's economy. More people will vacation at ski resorts and other travel destinations when they feel that travel is safe and the economy is strong. In bad economic times and periods of uncertainty, people will take fewer vacations. During this time, fewer employment opportunities may be available to workers in the ski resort industry.

FOR MORE INFORMATION

For information on employment opportunities and to fill out an online employment application, contact

Aspen Skiing Company
PO Box 1248
Aspen, CO 81612
Tel: 800-308-6935
Email: ascconcierge@aspensnowmass.com
http://www.aspensnowmass.com

For industry information, contact
National Ski Areas Association
133 South Van Gordon Street, Suite 300
Lakewood, CO 80228
Tel: 303-987-1111
Email: nsaa@nsaa.org
http://www.nsaa.org

*For information on the ski industry and ski instructor certification,
contact*
Professional Ski Instructors of America
133 South Van Gordon Street, Suite 101
Lakewood, CO 80228
Tel: 303-987-9390
http://www.psia.org

*The University of Maine at Farmington offers the ski industries
certificate program. This specialized program combines a bachelor's
degree with a certificate concentration in the ski industry. For more
information, contact*
University of Maine at Farmington
Ski Industries Certificate Program
111 South Street
Farmington, ME 04938
Tel: 207-778-7385
Email: ebreiden@maine.edu
http://ski.umf.maine.edu

*For information on employment, travel packages, and resort news,
visit*
SkiResorts.Com
http://www.skiresorts.com

Spa Attendants

OVERVIEW

Spa attendants work in hotels, resorts, and salons. They are specially trained in facial, body, and water treatments. They assist massage therapists and estheticians, and prepare and clean the treatment rooms and tables. They provide spa customers with refreshments, towels, washcloths, and robes. According to the International SPA Association, there are 282,000 people employed by the more than 9,600 spas in the United States.

HISTORY

Fossils prove that even the mammoths of over 20,000 years ago enjoyed a good spa treatment. The town of Hot Springs, a small resort village nestled in the hills of South Dakota, features a fossil excavation site; this site serves as evidence that mammoths were attracted to the area's pools of warm water. Humans share this attraction. Native Americans considered natural hot springs to be sacred healing grounds. All through Europe, the ancient Romans built colossal spas, including the Baths of Caracalla, one of the seven wonders of the world. Only its ruins remain, but Caracalla once featured hot and cold baths, a swimming pool, a gymnasium, shops, art galleries, and acres of gardens.

Although spas fell out of favor during the Middle Ages, by the 17th and 18th centuries they had once again become popular in Europe. An interest in making use of natural resources for healing and relaxation spread, and by the late 1800s there was hardly a well of natural spring water in the United States that a businessman hadn't capitalized upon. At the turn of the century in the United

School Subjects
Chemistry
Health

Personal Skills
Communication/ideas
Helping/teaching

Work Environment
Primarily indoors
Primarily one location

Minimum Education Level
High school diploma

Salary Range
$12,000 to $21,000 to $30,000

Certification or Licensing
None available

Outlook
Faster than the average

DOT
N/A

GOE
N/A

NOC
N/A

O*NET-SOC
N/A

The Roots of Today's Spa Experience

Public baths date back over 4,500 years. They have been found in Pakistan, ancient Babylon, and Egypt. The medieval Turks created the five stages of the spa bath still practiced today: dry heat, moist heat, massage, cold, and rest. Some cultural contributions to the spa experience have gained popularity more than others: Asian and European massages and whirlpools are all the stuff of the modern-day spa; the Finnish sauna practice of beating one another with tree branches, however, has failed to take the world by storm.

States, people visited resorts and spas (with or without natural hot springs) for exercise and relaxation. By the 1920s spas had become popular retreats for the wealthy. Since that time, spas have diversified their services and attracted a wide range of visitors. Today's spas have clients ranging from busy professionals looking for several hours of stress reduction, to families looking for healthy vacations, to pregnant women seeking relaxation, to men looking to keep fit. According to the International SPA Association, there were more than 156 million spa visits in the United States in 2001.

THE JOB

From the ylang-ylang plant to the lomilomi massage, spa attendants are teaching vacationers a new language of health and rejuvenation. Although there were only 30 spas in the United States in the late 1970s, the number now has grown past 9,000. More than 7,000 of these are day spas, where clients can check in for an afternoon of relaxation and rejuvenation. The remainder are resort/hotel spas, which welcome clients for longer visits. Spas and resorts have cropped up around natural hot springs, the seaside, the desert, the mountains, and even the plains. Some spas are designed to meet very specific needs, such as weight management and holistic wellness. While most spas offer the usual facials, body wraps, and massages, many are expanding to include "mind/body awareness" as people flock to spas for both physical and spiritual needs. In some spas, you can schedule hypnosis, yoga, and dream therapy sessions right after your horseback riding, tennis game, and round of golf. So the duties of a spa attendant can vary greatly from location to location. Spa attendants are also finding work outside of the vacation industry, at salons and day spas, as cosmetologists recognize the need to expand into other areas of beauty care. In addition to actually performing treatments, spa attendants devise special treatment plans for individual clients. They also schedule appointments, order and sell products, launder linens, and clean all spa areas. They offer advice on treatments and skin care products.

Craig Rabago works as a men's spa technician for the Ihilani Resort and Spa in Kapolei, Hawaii. *Ihilani* means "heavenly splendor," and it is part of Rabago's job to help guests realize this splendor. "I create an atmosphere that is heavenly for them," Rabago explains. "I'm of Hawaiian descent and a local. I give people a warm welcome and make them feel at home." Rabago has been trained in a variety of services, including seaweed wraps, salt scrubs, and thalasso hydrotherapy (a fresh seawater massage). The Ihilani features a fitness center and separate spas for men and women; each spa includes a sauna, steam room, needle shower, hot tub, and cold plunge. For the popular "cool ti leaf wrap," Rabago prepares a table in one of the spa's private rooms, spreading out the long, frond-like Hawaiian ti leaves and treating them with special oils. When the guest arrives for his wrap, Rabago gives him a robe and sandals and shows him to the lockers and then the showers. When the guest is ready for the treatment, Rabago then brings him to the treatment room and directs him to lie back on the table. As he explains the treatment, Rabago rubs the guest's skin with oils and lotions, making sure to pay special attention to sunburn, dry skin, and other trouble areas. He then wraps the guest in a damp sheet. Rabago leaves him wrapped for 25 minutes, checking in occasionally to make sure the guest is comfortable. In between treatments, Rabago must take linen inventory and keep the spa areas clean. He also does a fair amount of work on the computer. "But taking care of the guests' needs—that's my priority," Rabago says.

The Ihilani capitalizes on its locale, providing treatments with fresh seawater, sea salt, seaweed, and Hawaiian plants. In a different kind of environment, a spa and resort may provide very different services. Mud baths, natural hot spring whirlpools, volcanic mineral treatment—resort owners around the world develop their spas with the natural surroundings in mind. This results in very specific training for spa attendants. "The training was time-consuming," Rabago recalls. "The spa techs train with each other. We put in lots of hours of practice before we actually go to work on a guest."

REQUIREMENTS

High School

To prepare for work as a spa attendant, take high school courses in anatomy, physiology, and biology. These classes will give you an understanding of the human body and muscle systems. Chemistry will prepare you for the use and preparation of skin care products. Health courses will teach you about nutrition, fitness, and other issues of importance to the health-conscious patrons of resorts and spas. Because so many spas offer treatment for both the body and the mind, take some psychology courses to learn about the history of treating depression, anxiety, and other mental and emotional problems. Finally, take computer classes, which will allow you to become comfortable using this technology. If in your future job you need to keep track of spa supplies, you will probably be using a computer to do so.

In addition to these classes, you will benefit from having CPR and first aid training. Check with your high school to find out if it offers such training or contact organizations such as your local Red Cross. Many spas require attendants to know CPR and first aid, and your training will give you an advantage when looking for a job. Currently no specific postsecondary training program exists for spa attendants. Most spas put new hires through their own attendant training programs. Any work experience that you already have in a spa, therefore, will make you an appealing job candidate. During your high school years, try to get a summer job at one of the many resorts across the country. Spas often hire extra help to deal with the increased number of guests during this peak vacation period. Although you may only be working with the laundry, you will have the opportunity to see how a spa or resort is run and find out about the many different jobs available.

Some spas require their attendants to be certified cosmeticians or massage therapists. In such cases, education beyond high school is required. If you know of a specific spa at which you wish to work, ask about the hiring policy for attendants. Cosmeticians receive their training from cosmetology schools; massage therapists are educated at schools of massage therapy. Licensing requirements for these professionals vary by state, and you should know what these requirements are before you begin a program of study.

Other Requirements

Craig Rabago of the Ihilani advises that a good spa attendant should "be happy, courageous, and ambitious." Guests of resorts and spas expect to be pampered and welcomed and can only fully relax during a spa treatment if the attendant is calm and considerate. Be prepared to serve your clients and to remain friendly and helpful. "But don't be timid and shy," Rabago says. "This is a good way to meet people from all around the world. You can broaden your horizons."

Any shyness and excessive modesty may also prevent you from performing your spa duties properly. You'll be applying lotions and oils to the naked skin of your guests—if you are uncomfortable, your clients will detect it and become uncomfortable themselves. You must take a professional approach so that your clients feel safe and at ease. You should have a good "bedside manner"—the calm, comforting approach health care professionals use. Self-confidence is also important; you must convey to your client that you're knowledgeable about the treatment.

EXPLORING

One of the best ways to explore this type of work is to get a part-time or summer job at a spa. You may be surprised by the number of spas in your area. There may even be a resort on the outskirts of your city. Look in the yellow pages under "Beauty Salons and Services" as well as "Health Clubs" and "Massage." (Many of the listings under "Spa" are only for hot tub dealerships.) Visit a salon or day spa and ask to interview someone who works as a spa attendant. Some attendants may allow you to shadow them for a day or two. Larger salons may have openings for part-time attendants, allowing you to gather firsthand experience.

Many resorts across the country advertise nationally for summer help. Check the classifieds of vacation and travel magazines, and visit http://www.resortjobs.com for a listing. You could also select a resort and spa from the pages of a tourism publication, such as *Resorts and Great Hotels* (http://www.resortsgreathotels.com), and call the hotel directly to request information about summer jobs. *Spa Finder* (http://www.spafinders.com) magazine also publishes a directory of spas.

If you are unable to find a job at a spa, consider a part-time or summer job at a local hotel, beauty salon, or tanning salon. In any of these locations you will gain experience working with guests and providing for their comfort. Nursing homes and hospitals also employ high school students to provide clients or patients with personal care services. Working at a retail store specializing in products for skin care and beauty, aromatherapy, and massage can teach you about various spa treatments and products and help you decide if you are interested in this line of work.

If you have the money, consider making an appointment for yourself at a spa in your area. You may not be able to afford a vacation or full-day treatment, but even an hour spent as a client at a spa can give you an impression of what working in such an environment would be like.

EMPLOYERS

The International SPA Association estimates that, as of 2002, 282,000 people worked in the spa industry in the United States, which is up from 151,000 in 1999. Spas have grown at a very rapid rate over the past five years, and they should continue to do so as more people begin to value the benefits of spa visits. The primary employers of spa attendants are hotels, resorts, salons, and, naturally, spas. Increasing numbers of salons are adding spas to their facilities to maintain a competitive edge; this will lead to increased opportunities for spa attendants throughout the country, mostly in larger cities and metropolitan areas. The same is true for hotel spas. Many spas, however, are clustered in resort areas with attractions like hot springs and consistently pleasant climates.

STARTING OUT

Many spa attendants receive their training on the job, but some background experience in health care or cosmetology may help you in landing that first job as a spa attendant. Craig Rabago, for example, worked as a surgical aide before going to work for the Ihilani. "The work is related," he said, "but it's a very different atmosphere." He learned about the spa job from a listing in the newspaper. If you're not particular about your geographic location, check travel publications for listings of resorts and spas, or visit http://www. spafinders.com on the Web, and contact the spas about job openings. *Spa Finder,* both online and in their print directory, lists spas according to their specialties and locations.

A degree from a cosmetology or massage therapy school can be valuable when looking for a job in a spa. Many of these degree programs require field work, or hands-on experience, and will put you in touch with salons and fitness centers. Without a degree, you may be limited in the spa treatments you're allowed to perform. But as more and more individual hair stylists and beauty salons open day spas to accommodate all the needs of their clients, both licensed and unlicensed spa attendants will find more job opportunities.

ADVANCEMENT

The longer an attendant works in a spa, the more he or she will learn about the services provided there. The attendant will also have more opportunities to expand upon the on-the-job training and potentially be allowed to perform more treatments. Though attendants typically start off with only an hourly wage, they can eventually receive commissions and tips. The more guests an attendant works with, the better tips and commission he or she will make. In a salon or day spa situation, the clientele will include regular customers. If they are happy with an attendant's work, they will request that attendant's services specifically and thus increase the attendant's income.

Attendants who complete further formal education also become qualified for more advanced positions. Those who attend cosmetology school to become cosmeticians typically have classes such as anatomy, chemistry, and physiology. They are qualified to work on the skin, giving facials, body wraps, and makeup applications, and may also do hair removal by waxing or plucking. Nail technician programs offered through cosmetology schools or nail schools qualify the graduate to give manicures and pedicures. Attendants who are particularly interested in fitness may want to consider advancement by getting an associate's degree from a fitness program. Courses for such programs include muscle conditioning, nutrition, and injury prevention. Those interested in massage may seek advancement by completing a massage therapy school program, which will qualify them to give different types of massage. These programs include course work in anatomy and physiology as well as provide hands-on training.

Some attendants advance to become spa program directors. As program directors, they are responsible for adding new services, training spa attendants, determining what skin products to use, and controlling other details of the spa's daily practices. Those who wish to run their own business may eventually open their own spa.

EARNINGS

Salaries for spa attendants vary greatly across the country, so no significant salary survey has been conducted in recent years. Spa attendants make from minimum wage to around $10 per hour. Salaries vary according to work environment (a large resort will pay more than a small salon) and the spa attendant's responsibilities. Spa attendants are either paid by the hour or by commission (a percentage of the spa treatments performed). Spa attendants also receive tips of between 10 and 15 percent. Some spas automatically bill guests an additional percentage to cover the tip, so that the guest doesn't have to worry about having the money on hand to give to the attendant. With tips from a wealthy clientele and a commission on higher priced services, a spa attendant at a fine hotel will make much more than an attendant in a smaller day spa. Employees of spas are likely to receive better benefits than many of their counterparts in the cosmetology field. Spa attendants working at hotels may also receive a variety of perks, such as discounted spa treatments, guest rooms, meals in the hotel restaurants, and travel packages.

WORK ENVIRONMENT

Working among vacationers in a sunny, scenic part of the world can be very enjoyable. Most spa attendants work within well-decorated, temperature-controlled buildings, with soothing music piped through the speaker systems. Fresh fruit, tea, and other refreshments are often readily available. Spa attendants work directly with a public that has come to a resort to alleviate stress and other worries, making for very relaxed interactions. Some hotel spa attendants even live on the premises in special employee quarters, or in nearby housing, allowing them to live close to the beaches, mountains, or whatever natural beauty surrounds the resort.

Because spas usually open in the wee hours of the morning and close after dark, spa attendants may have to work long, irregular hours. Depending on the codes of the spa, they wear uniforms and jackets. They also wear gloves if their skin is sensitive to some of the products.

In a local beauty salon, a spa attendant tries to maintain a similarly relaxed environment in the few rooms dedicated to spa treatment. The rest of the salon, however, may be noisy with waiting customers, hair dryers, electric clippers, and music. The salon may also affect those with allergies to chemicals in hair treatment products.

Day spas, which may be located in large cities, typically strive to maintain a serene environment for the clientele, from the reception area, where soft music may be playing in the background, to the private treatment rooms, which may have soft lighting. While the spa attendant may work in these areas, he or she is also part of the activity behind the scenes, often working with damp laundry, cleaning supplies, and spa products.

OUTLOOK

The International SPA Association reports that spa visits are on the rise in the United States, with clients making nearly 156 million spa visits in 2001 alone. This increase can be attributed to the growing appreciation for the benefits of spa visits, the increased number of day spas, and increased popularity of spas among men. In fact, many spas are adding treatments specifically for men. These expanding facilities and new treatment options should translate into job opportunities for everyone working in this industry, including spa attendants.

In addition, the public is becoming more health conscious, and people are looking to spas for both enjoyable and educational vacations. Some spas are specializing in teaching guests new patterns of diet, exercise, and skin care. A number of health care professionals are even predicting that spas will be covered by health insurance plans; doctors will write prescriptions to patients for spa treatments. To compete with other spas, and to satisfy returning guests, spas are likely to offer even more diverse lists of services and treatments. The spa attendant will have to keep ahead of health and beauty trends and be capable of adapting to new programs and methods.

Anticipating a future of one-stop beauty treatment, the owners of hair and beauty salons are dedicating rooms to spa treatments. For the cost of a little remodeling, hair salons can stay competitive with local day spas, as well as generate more business. Spa attendants may find their best job opportunities at these salons, where they can earn a good commission and establish a client base.

FOR MORE INFORMATION

For employment opportunities, contact
Day Spa Association
310 17th Street
Union City, NJ 07087
Tel: 201-865-2065
http://www.dayspaassociation.com

Spa Salon Staffing Services
PO Box 6831
Mesa, AZ 85216-6831
Tel: 888-736-1711
http://www.spasalonstaffing.com

For more information on the spa industry, contact
International Spa Association
2365 Harrodsburg Road, Suite A325
Lexington, KY 40504
Tel: 888-651-4772
http://www.experienceispa.com

For information on accredited cosmetology schools and financial aid, contact

National Accrediting Commission of Cosmetology Arts and Sciences
4401 Ford Avenue, Suite 1300
Alexandria, VA 22302-1432
Tel: 703-600-7600
http://www.naccas.org

Tour Guides

OVERVIEW

Tour guides plan and oversee travel arrangements and accommodations for groups of tourists. They assist travelers with questions or problems, and they may provide travelers with itineraries of their proposed travel route and plans. Tour guides research their destinations thoroughly so that they can handle any unforeseen situation that may occur. There are approximately 38,000 tour and travel guides employed in the United States.

HISTORY

People have always had a certain fascination with the unknown. Curiosity about distant cities and foreign cultures was one of the main forces behind the spread of civilization. Traveling in the ancient world was an arduous and sometimes dangerous task. Today, however, travel is commonplace. People travel for business, recreation, and education. Schoolchildren may take field trips to their state's capitol, and some college students now have the opportunity to study in foreign countries. Recreation and vacation travel account for much of people's spending of their disposable income.

QUICK FACTS

School Subjects
Foreign language
History
Speech

Personal Skills
Communication/ideas
Leadership/management

Work Environment
Indoors and outdoors
Primarily multiple locations

Minimum Education Level
Some postsecondary training

Salary Range
$13,040 to $18,790 to
$45,000+

Certification or Licensing
Recommended

Outlook
About as fast as the average

DOT
353

GOE
11.02.01

NOC
6441

O*NET-SOC
39-6022.00

Early travelers were often accompanied by guides who had become familiar with the routes on earlier trips. When leisure travel became more commonplace in the 19th century, women and young children were not expected to travel alone, so relatives or house servants often acted as companions. Today, tour guides act as escorts for people visiting foreign countries and provide them with additional information on interesting facets of life in another part of the world. In a way, tour guides have taken the place of the early scouts, acting as experts in settings and situations that other people find unfamiliar.

THE JOB

Acting as knowledgeable companions and chaperons, tour guides escort groups of tourists to different cities and countries. Their job is to make sure that the passengers in a group tour enjoy an interesting and safe trip. To do this, they have to know a great deal about their travel destination and about the interests, knowledge, and expectations of the people on the tour.

One basic responsibility of tour guides is handling all the details of a trip prior to departure. They may schedule airline flights, bus trips, or train trips as well as book cruises, house boats, or car rentals. They also research area hotels and other lodging for the group and make reservations in advance. If anyone in the group has unique requirements, such as a specialized diet or a need for wheelchair accessibility, the tour guide will work to meet these requests.

Tour guides plan itineraries and daily activities, keeping in mind the interests of the group. For example, a group of music lovers visiting Vienna may wish to see the many sites of musical history there as well as attend a performance by that city's orchestra. In addition to sightseeing tours, guides may make arrangements in advance for special exhibits, dining experiences, and side trips. Alternate outings are sometimes planned in case of inclement weather conditions.

The second major responsibility of tour guides is, of course, the tour itself. Here, they must make sure all aspects of transportation, lodging, and recreation meet the planned itinerary. They must see to it that travelers' baggage and personal belongings are loaded and handled properly. If the tour includes meals and trips to local establishments, the guide must make sure that each passenger is on time for the various arrivals and departures.

Tour guides provide the people in their groups with interesting information on the locale and alert them to special sights. Tour guides become familiar with the history and significance of places through research and previous visits and endeavor to make the visit as entertaining and informative as possible. They may speak the native language or hire an interpreter in order to get along well with the local people. They are also familiar with local customs so their group will not offend anyone unknowingly. They see that the group stays together so that members do not miss their transportation arrangements or get lost. Guides may also arrange free time for travelers to pursue their individual interests, although time frames and common meeting points for regrouping are established in advance.

Even with thorough preparation, unexpected occurrences can arise on any trip and threaten to ruin everyone's good time. Tour guides must be resourceful to handle these surprises, such as when points of interest are closed or accommodations turn out to be unacceptable. They must be familiar with an area's resources so that they can help in emergencies such as passenger illness or lost personal items. Tour guides often intercede on their travelers' behalf when any questions or problems arise regarding currency, restaurants, customs, or necessary identification.

REQUIREMENTS

High School
Although as a tour guide you will not necessarily need a college education, you should at least have a high school diploma. Courses such as speech, communications, art, sociology, anthropology, political science, and literature often prove beneficial. Some tour guides study foreign languages and cultures as well as geography, history, and architecture.

Postsecondary Training
Some cities have professional schools that offer curricula in the travel industry. Such training may take nine to 12 months and offer job placement services. Some two- and four-year colleges offer tour guide training that lasts six to eight weeks. Community colleges may offer programs in tour escort training. Programs such as these often may be taken on a part-time basis. Classes may include history, world geography, psychology, human relations, and communication courses. Sometimes students go on field trips themselves to gain experience. Some travel agencies and tour companies offer their own training so that their tour guides may receive instruction that complements the tour packages the company offers.

Certification or Licensing
The National Tour Association offers the certified tour professional designation to candidates who complete 200 education credits in two areas: professional study and professional activity. Candidates must also have a minimum of five years of employment in the travel industry, unless they have an industry-specific degree from an accredited

college or university. Candidates with a college degree must have a minimum of three years of industry employment.

Other Requirements

To be a tour guide, you should be an outgoing, friendly, and confident person. You must be aware of the typical travelers' needs and the kinds of questions and concerns travelers might have. As a tour guide, you should be comfortable being in charge of large groups of people and have good time-management skills. You also need to be resourceful and be able to adapt to different environments. Tour guides are fun-loving and know how to make others feel at ease in unfamiliar surroundings. Tour guides should enjoy working with people as much as they enjoy traveling.

EXPLORING

One way to become more familiar with the responsibilities of this job is to accompany local tours. Many cities have their own historical societies and museums that offer tours as well as opportunities to volunteer. To appreciate what is involved with speaking in front of groups and the kind of research that may be necessary for leading tours, you can prepare speeches or presentations for class or local community groups. You may also find it helpful to read publications such as *Courier* (http://www.ntaonline.com), the National Tour Association's monthly travel magazine.

EMPLOYERS

The major employers of tour guides are, naturally, tour companies. Many tour guides work on a freelance basis, while others may own their own tour businesses. Approximately 38,000 tour and travel guides are employed in the United States.

STARTING OUT

If you are interested in a career as a tour guide, you may begin as a guide for a museum or state park. This would be a good introduction to handling groups of people, giving lectures on points of interest or exhibits and developing confidence and leadership qualities. Zoos, theme parks, historical sites, or local walking tours often need volunteers or part-time employees to work in their information centers, offer visitors directions, and answer a variety of inquiries. When openings occur, it is common for part-time workers to move into full-time positions.

Travel agencies, tour bus companies, and park districts often need additional help during the summer months when the travel season is in full swing. Societies and organizations for architecture and natural history, as well as other cultural groups, often train and employ guides. If you are interested in working as a tour guide for one of these types of groups, you should submit your application directly to the directors of personnel or managing directors.

ADVANCEMENT

Tour guides gain experience by handling more complicated trips. Some workers may advance through specialization, such as tours to specific countries or to multiple destinations. Some tour guides choose to open their own travel agencies or work for wholesale tour companies, selling trip packages to individuals or retail tour companies.

Some tour guides become *travel writers* and report on exotic destinations for magazines and newspapers. Other guides may decide to work in the corporate world and plan travel arrangements for company executives. With the further development of the global economy, many different jobs have become available for people who know foreign languages and cultures.

EARNINGS

Tour guides may find that they have peak and slack periods of the year that correspond to vacation and travel seasons. Many tour guides, however, work eight months of the year. Salaries range from $6.27 per hour to $22 per hour. Experienced guides with managerial responsibilities can earn up to $65,000 a year, including gratuities. According to the National Tour Association's *2000 Wage and Benefits Survey,* the average daily rate of compensation for tour directors/escorts was $113, a 25 percent increase since 1995.

Guides receive their meals and accommodations free while conducting a tour, in addition to a daily stipend to cover their personal expenses. Salaries and benefits vary, depending on the tour operators that employ guides and the location in which they are employed. Generally, the Great Lakes, Mid-Atlantic, Southeast, and Southern regions of the United States offer the highest compensation.

Tour guides often receive paid vacations as part of their fringe benefits package; some may also receive sick pay and health insurance. Some companies may offer profit sharing and bonuses. Guides often receive discounts from hotels, airlines, and transportation companies in appreciation for repeat business.

WORK ENVIRONMENT

The key word in the tour guide profession is variety. Most tour guides work in offices while they make travel arrangements and handle general business, but once on the road, they experience a wide range of accommodations, conditions, and situations. Tours to distant cities involve maneuvering through busy and confusing airports. Side trips may involve bus rides, train transfers, or private car rentals, all with varying degrees of comfort and reliability. Package trips that encompass seeing a number of foreign countries may require the guide to speak a different language in each city.

The constant feeling of being on the go and the responsibility of leading a large group of people can sometimes be stressful. Unexpected events and uncooperative people have the capacity to ruin part of a trip for everyone involved, including the guide. However, the thrill of travel, discovery, and meeting new people can be so rewarding that all the negatives can be forgotten (or eliminated by preplanning on the next trip).

OUTLOOK

Because of the many different travel opportunities for business, recreation, and education, there will be a steady need for tour guides through 2014. Tours designed for special interests, such as to ecologically significant areas and wilderness destinations, continue to grow in popularity. Although certain seasons are more popular for travel than others, well-trained tour guides can keep busy all year long.

Another area of tourism that is on the upswing is inbound tourism. Many foreign travelers view the United States as a dream destination, with tourist spots such as New York, Disney World, and our national park system drawing millions of foreign visitors each year. Job opportunities in inbound tourism will likely be more plentiful than those guiding Americans in foreign locations. The best opportunities in inbound tourism are in large cities with international airports and in areas with a large amount of tourist traffic. Opportunities will also be better for those guides who speak foreign languages.

Aspiring tour guides should keep in mind that this field is highly competitive. Tour guide jobs, because of the obvious benefits, are highly sought after, and the beginning job seeker may find it difficult to break into the business. It is important to remember that the travel and tourism industry is affected by the overall economy. When the economy is depressed, people have less money to spend and, therefore, they travel less. Recent terrorist attacks have also adversely affected the travel and tourism industry. If the public perceives that travel is risky, they will travel less and, as a result, tour guides may see reduced employment opportunities.

FOR MORE INFORMATION

For information on the travel industry and the related career of travel agent, contact
    American Society of Travel Agents
    1101 King Street, Suite 200
    Alexandria, VA 22314
    Tel: 703-739-2782
    Email: askasta@astahq.com
    http://www.astanet.com

For information on internships, scholarships, the certified tour professional designation, and a list of colleges and universities that offer tourism-related programs, contact
    National Tour Association
    546 East Main Street
    Lexington, KY 40508
    Tel: 800-682-8886
    Email: questions@ntastaff.com
    http://www.ntaonline.com

INTERVIEW

Georgette Blau founded and operates On Location Tours in New York City. The company provides tours of famous film and television sites in an around Manhattan. Georgette spoke with the editors of Careers in Focus: Travel & Hospitality *about her career and the tourism industry in general. For more information, visit http://www.sceneontv.com.*

Q. How and when did you decide to start a tour company?
A. It all happened by accident. In the fall of 1998, I was walking in my Upper East Side neighborhood one day, and I spotted the apartment building used in the opening credits of the television show *The Jeffersons.* When I went home that day, I looked into a book I had on TV locations. About six months later, I started a tour company called Scene on TV, which a year later was incorporated into On Location Tours.

Q. What kinds of tours do you offer? Is one season busier than others?

A. We only offer TV and movie location tours. Right now, in New York, we have three bus tours—The Manhattan TV and Movie tour (which includes locations from *Friends, Seinfeld, Spider-Man, Hitch,* and much more), the *Sex and the City* tour, and the *Sopranos* tour—and one walking tour, the Central Park Movie tour. Summer and the December holiday season are generally our busiest times. The *Sex and the City* tour right now is our most popular. There are many highlights to each tour, including "hop-offs" to get a closer look at locations. Two years ago on the *Sex and the City* tour we spotted Kyle MacLachlan [an actor from the show] at one of the stops on the tour. It was amazing. About 52 women from the tour ran after him (the two or so guys on the bus waited behind). I thought it was going to be for an autograph, but in fact it was to yell at him about how he had treated the character Charlotte on the show! I guess people confuse fiction and reality.

Q. What does a typical workday involve?

A. A typical workday is both fun and stressful, as it includes overseeing many different aspects of the business—operations, marketing, sales, and management. A lot of the day consists of emails and phone calls, talking to tour guides about concerns, helping with scheduling buses and tour guides, pitching the press, brainstorming marketing ideas, talking to the bus company about bus maintenance, and keeping up with sales. The work never ends! Thankfully we have a team that includes tour guides, sales, operations, marketing, and a concierge contact.

Q. What would you say are the pros and cons of running a tour company?

A. Tours are busier in certain seasons, so you have to go with the ebb and flow of the seasons, weather, and current events. Running bus tours in a city is somewhat of a challenge (dealing with the city, streets, neighborhoods, etc.) Tourism, however, is a leisure field, making it a lot of fun.

Q. What would you say are the most important skills and personal qualities for someone interested in pursuing this type of career? What is a good way to get started/gain experience?

A. Tourism is an extremely outgoing field, so the individual should be very outgoing, good at networking, and good at handling the public/customer service. A great way to get started in the business is by internships and by contacting the tourism associations (such as the National Tour Association—they even have scholarships). It's important when looking for an internship to make sure that it will offer well-rounded projects, not just the same administrative task on a daily basis.

Q. What advice do you have for someone who is interested in pursuing this type of career?
A. You really have to love travel and working with the public. In certain fields of tourism incomes are not very high, so an individual really has to enjoy his or her job! And with the travel industry changing so drastically, you have to be Internet-marketing savvy and able to think outside of the box.

Travel Agents

OVERVIEW

Travel agents assist individuals or groups who will be traveling by planning their itineraries, making transportation, hotel, and tour reservations, obtaining or preparing tickets, and performing related services. There are over 103,000 travel agents employed in the United States.

HISTORY

The first travel agency in the United States was established in 1872. Before this time, travel as an activity was not widespread, due to wars and international barriers, inadequate transportation and hotels, lack of leisure, the threat of contagious disease, and lower standards of living. Despite the glamour attached to such early travelers as Marco Polo, people of the Middle Ages and the 17th and 18th centuries were not accustomed to traveling for pleasure.

The manufacturing operations that started in the industrial revolution caused international trade to expand greatly. Commercial traffic between countries stimulated both business and personal travel. Yet until the 20th century, travel was arduous, and most areas were unprepared for tourists.

The travel business began with Thomas Cook, an Englishman who first popularized the guided tour. In 1841, Cook arranged his first excursion: a special Midland Counties Railroad Company train to carry passengers from Leicester to a temperance meeting in Loughborough. His business grew rapidly. He made arrangements for 165,000 visitors to attend the Great Exhibition of 1851 in London. The following year, he organized the first "Cook's Tour." Earnest groups of English tourists were soon seen traveling by camel to view the Pyramids and the Sphinx, gliding past historic castles on the Rhine, and riding by carriage to view the wonders of Paris. The "Grand Tour" of Europe soon became an integral part of a young person's education among the privileged classes.

Over the next century, the development of the railroads, the replacement of sailing ships with faster steamships, the advent of the automobile and the bus, and the invention of the airplane provided an improved quality of transportation that encouraged people to travel for relaxation and personal enrichment. At the same time, cities, regions, and countries began to appreciate the economic aspects of travel. Promotional campaigns were organized to attract and accommodate tourists. Formal organization of the travel industry was reflected in the establishment in 1931 of the American Society of Travel Agents.

In the past decade, travel agents have accommodated a great increase in family travel. This increase is in part a result of greater leisure time. As long as leisure time continues to grow and the nation's standard of living increases, there will be a need for travel agents to help people in planning their vacations wisely.

THE JOB

The travel agent may work as a salesperson, travel consultant, tour organizer, travel guide, bookkeeper, or small business executive. If the agent operates a one-person office, he or she usually performs all of these functions. Other travel agents work in offices with dozens of employees, which allows them to specialize in certain areas. In such offices, one staff member may become an authority on sea cruises, another may work on trips to the Far East, and a third may develop an extensive knowledge of either low-budget or luxury trips. In some cases, travel agents are employed by national or international firms and can draw upon very extensive resources.

As salespeople, travel agents must be able to motivate people to take advantage of their services. Travel agents study their customers' interests, learn where they have traveled, appraise their financial resources and available time, and present a selection of travel options. Customers are then able to choose how and where they want to travel with a minimum of effort.

Travel agents consult a variety of published and computer-based sources for information on air transportation departure and arrival times, airfares, and hotel ratings and accommodations. They often base their recommendations on their own travel experiences or those of colleagues or clients. Travel agents may visit hotels, resorts, and restaurants to rate their comfort, cleanliness, and quality of food and service.

As travel consultants, agents give their clients suggestions regarding travel plans and itineraries, information on transportation alternatives, and advice on the available accommodations and rates of hotels and motels. They also explain and help with passport and visa regulations, foreign currency and exchange, climate and wardrobe, health requirements, customs regulations, baggage and accident insurance, traveler's checks or letters of credit, car rentals, tourist attractions, and welcome or tour services.

Many travel agents only sell tours that are developed by other organizations. The most skilled agents, however, often organize tours on a wholesale basis. This involves developing an itinerary, contracting a knowledgeable person to lead the tour, making tentative reservations for transportation, hotels, and side trips, publicizing the tour through descriptive brochures, advertisements, and other travel agents, scheduling reservations, and handling last-minute problems. Sometimes tours are arranged at the specific request of a group or to meet a client's particular needs.

In addition to other duties, travel agents may serve as *tour guides*, leading trips ranging from one week to six months to locations around the world. Agents often find tour leadership a useful way to gain personal travel experience. It also gives them the chance to become thoroughly acquainted with the people in the tour group, who may then use the agent to arrange future trips or recommend the agent to friends and relatives. Tour leaders are usually reimbursed for all their expenses or receive complimentary transportation and lodging. Most travel agents, however, arrange for someone to cover for them at work during their absence, which may make tour leadership prohibitive for self-employed agents.

Agents serve as bookkeepers to handle the complex pattern of transportation and hotel reservations that each trip entails. They work directly with airline, steamship, railroad, bus, and car rental companies. They make direct contact with hotels and sightseeing organizations or work indirectly through a receptive operator in the city involved. These arrangements require a great deal of accuracy because mistakes could result in a client being left stranded in a foreign or remote area. After reservations are made, agents write up or obtain tickets, write out itineraries, and send out bills for the reservations involved. They also send out confirmations to airlines, hotels, and other companies.

Travel agents must promote their services. They present slides or movies to social and special interest groups, arrange advertising displays, and suggest company-sponsored trips to business managers.

REQUIREMENTS

High School

A high school diploma is the minimum requirement for becoming a travel agent. If you are interested in pursuing a career as an agent, be certain to include some computer courses, as well as typing or key-boarding courses, in your class schedule. Since much of your work as a travel agent will involve computerized reservation systems, it is important to have basic keyboarding skills and to be comfortable working with computers.

Because being able to communicate clearly with clients is central to this job, any high school course that enhances communication skills, such as English or speech, is a good choice. Proficiency in a foreign language, while not a requirement, might be helpful in many cases, such as when you are working with international travelers. Finally, geography, social studies, and business mathematics are classes that may also help prepare you for various aspects of the travel agent's work.

You can also begin learning about being a travel agent while still in high school by getting a summer or part-time job in travel and tourism. D. G. Elmore, president of Gant Travel, a national chain of corporate travel agencies, suggests that interested high school students find a job in a travel agency, doing whatever they can do. "I would advise them to get a job doing anything from tearing down tickets to delivering tickets. Anything that brings them in contact with the business will go a long way toward getting them a job," he says. "If they did that their senior year in high school in a major city, they'd have a job by the end of the summer, almost certainly." If finding a part-time or summer job in a travel agency proves impos-sible, you might consider looking for a job as a reservation agent for an airline, rental car agency, or hotel.

Postsecondary Training

Travel courses are available from certain colleges, private vocational schools, and adult education programs in public high schools. Some colleges and universities grant bachelor's and master's degrees in travel and tourism. Although college training is not required for work as a travel agent, it can be very helpful and is expected to become increasingly important. It is predicted that in the future most agents will be college graduates. Travel schools provide basic reservation training and other training related to travel agents' func-tions, which is helpful but not required.

A liberal arts or business administration background is recom-mended for a career in this field. Useful liberal arts courses include foreign languages, geography, English, communications, history, anthropology, political science, art and music appreciation, and literature. Pertinent business courses include transportation, business law, hotel management, marketing, office management, and accounting. As in many other fields, computer skills are increasingly important.

Certification or Licensing

To be able to sell passage on various types of transportation, you must be approved by the conferences of carriers involved. These are the Airlines Reporting Corporation, the International Air Transport Association, and the Cruise Lines International Association. To sell tickets for these individual conferences, you must be clearly established in the travel business and have a good personal and business background. Not all travel agents are authorized to sell passage by all of the above conferences. Naturally, if you wish to sell the widest range of services, you should seek affiliation with all four.

Currently, travel agents are not required to be federally licensed. The following states require some form of registration or licensing: California, Florida, Hawaii, Illinois, Iowa, Ohio, Oregon, Rhode Island, and Washington.

Travel agents may choose to become certified by the Institute of Certified Travel Agents (ICTA). The ICTA offers certification programs leading to the designations of certified travel associate (CTA) and certified travel counselor (CTC). In order to become a CTA, you must have 18 months of experience as a travel agent, complete a 12-course program, and pass a written test. In order to become a CTC, you must have five years of experience, have attained CTA status, take a 12-course program, and pass a final exam. While not a requirement, certification by ICTA will help you progress in your career.

The ICTA also offers travel agents a number of other programs such as sales skills development courses and destination specialist courses, which provide a detailed knowledge of various geographic regions of the world.

Other Requirements

The primary requisite for success in the travel field is a sincere interest in travel. Your knowledge of and travel experiences with major tourist centers, various hotels, and local customs and points of interest make you a more effective and convincing source of assistance. Yet the work of travel agents is not one long vacation. They operate in a highly competitive industry.

As a travel agent, you must be able to make quick and accurate use of transportation schedules and tariffs. You must be able to handle addition and subtraction quickly. Almost all agents make use of computers to get the very latest information on rates and schedules and to make reservations.

You will work with a wide range of personalities as a travel agent, so skills in psychology and diplomacy will be important for you to have. You must also be able to generate enthusiasm among your customers and be resourceful in solving any problems that might arise. Knowledge of foreign languages is useful because many customers come from other countries, and you will be in frequent contact with foreign hotels and travel agencies.

EXPLORING

Any type of part-time experience with a travel agency will be helpful if you're interested in pursuing this career. A small agency may welcome help during peak travel seasons or when an agent is away from the office. If your high school or college arranges career conferences, you may be able to invite a speaker from the travel industry. Visits to local travel agents will also provide you with helpful information.

If you are already pursuing a travel or hospitality career in college, you might also consider joining the Future Travel Professionals Club, organized by the American Society of Travel Agents (ASTA). Membership allows you to network with professional members of the ASTA, attend chapter meetings, be eligible for scholarships, and receive two newsletters. For more information contact the ASTA (see sources at the end of this article).

EMPLOYERS

There are about 103,000 travel agents employed in the United States. Agents may work for commercial travel agents, work in the corporate travel department of a large company, or be self-employed. Travel agencies employ more than 8 out of 10 salaried agents. About one-tenth of agents are self-employed.

In addition to the regular travel business, a number of travel jobs are available with oil companies, automobile clubs, and transportation companies. Some jobs in travel are on the staffs of state and local governments seeking to encourage tourism.

STARTING OUT

As you start searching for a career in the travel field, you may begin by working for a company involved with transportation and tourism. Fortunately, a number of positions exist that are particularly appropriate if you are young and have limited work experience. Airlines, for example, hire flight attendants, reservation agents, and ticket clerks. Railroads and cruise line companies also have clerical positions; the rise in their popularity in recent years has resulted in more job opportunities. Those with travel experience may secure positions as tour guides. Organizations and companies with extensive travel operations may hire employees whose main responsibility is making travel arrangements.

Since travel agencies tend to have relatively small staffs, most openings are filled as a result of direct application and personal contact. While evaluating the merits of various travel agencies, you may wish to note whether the agency's owner belongs to ASTA. This trade group may also help in several other ways. It sponsors adult night school courses in travel agency operation in some metropolitan areas. It also offers a 15-lesson travel agency correspondence course. Also available, for a modest charge, is a travel agency management kit containing information that is particularly helpful to if you are considering setting up your own agency. ASTA's publication *Travel News* includes a classified advertising section listing available positions and agencies for sale.

ADVANCEMENT

Advancement opportunities within the travel field are limited to growth in terms of business volume or extent of specialization. Successful agents, for example, may hire additional employees or set up branch offices. A travel agency worker who has held his or her position for a while may be promoted to become a *travel assistant*. Travel assistants are responsible for answering general questions about transportation, providing current costs of hotel accommodations, and providing other information.

Travel agents may also advance to work as a *corporate travel manager*. Corporate travel managers work for companies, not travel agencies. They book all business travel for a company's employees.

Travel bureau employees may decide to go into business for themselves. Agents may show their professional status by belonging to ASTA, which requires its members to have three years of satisfactory travel agent experience and approval by at least two carrier conferences.

EARNINGS

Travel agency income comes from commissions paid by hotels, car rental companies, cruise lines, and tour operators. Due to the rising popularity of Internet travel sites, which enable customers to book their own flights, airlines no longer pay commissions to travel agents. This has been a big blow to those in this career, and it is a trend that will probably continue.

Travel agents typically earn a straight salary. In 2004, salaries of travel agents ranged from $17,180 to $44,090, with an average of $27,640, according to the U.S. Department of Labor. In addition to experience level, the location of the firm is also a factor in how much travel agents earn. Agents working in larger metropolitan areas tend to earn more than their counterparts in smaller cities.

Small travel agencies provide a smaller-than-average number of fringe benefits such as retirement, medical, and life insurance plans. Self-employed agents tend to earn more than those who work for others, although the business risk is greater. Also, a self-employed agent may not see much money for the first year or two, since it often takes time to establish a client base that is large enough to make a profit. Those who own their own businesses may experience large fluctuations in income because the travel business is extremely sensitive to swings in the economy.

One of the benefits of working as a travel agent is the chance to travel at a discounted price. Major airlines offer special agent fares, which are often only 25 percent of regular cost. Hotels, car rental companies, cruise lines, and tour operators also offer reduced rates for travel agents. Agents also get the opportunity to take free or low-cost group tours sponsored by transportation carriers, tour operators, and cruise lines. These trips, called "fam" trips, are designed to familiarize agents with locations and accommodations so that agents can better market them to their clients.

WORK ENVIRONMENT

The job of the travel agent is not as simple or glamorous as might be expected. Travel is a highly competitive field. Since almost every travel agent can offer the client the same service, agents must depend on repeat customers for much of their business. Their reliability, courtesy, and effectiveness in past transactions will determine whether they will get repeat business.

Travel agents also work in an atmosphere of keen competition for referrals. They must resist direct or indirect pressure from travel-related companies that have provided favors in the past (free trips, for example) and book all trips based only on the best interests of clients.

Most agents work a 40-hour week, although this frequently includes working a half-day on Saturday or an occasional evening. During busy seasons (typically from January through June), overtime may be necessary. Agents may receive additional salary for this work or be given compensatory time off.

As they gain experience, agents become more effective. One study revealed that 98 percent of all agents had more than three years' experience in some form of the travel field. Almost half had 20 years or more in this area.

OUTLOOK

The U.S. Department of Labor predicts that employment of travel agents will decline through 2014. Most airlines and other travel suppliers now offer consumers the option of making their own travel arrangements through online reservation services, which are readily accessible through the Internet. Thus, travelers are becoming less dependent upon agents to make travel arrangements for them. The American Society of Travel Agents reports that approximately 21 million consumers were booking their travel arrangements exclusively online as of June 2002. Additionally, airlines have eliminated the flat commission they pay travel agencies. This has reduced the income of many agencies, thereby making them less profitable and less able to hire new travel agents. Since these innovations are recent, their full effect on travel agents has not yet been determined.

However, consumers should continue to spend more on travel and tourism over the next decade, which will help employment prospects for travel agents. There will also be many opportunities to plan tour services for foreign visitor vacationing in the United States, and to arrange frequent trips for businesses with overseas offices. Despite the challenges travel agents face, there are still many people who prefer their services over online booking, as they appreciate the efficiency, value, and face-to-face contact that travel agents provide.

FOR MORE INFORMATION

Visit the ASTA Web site to read the online pamphlet Becoming a Travel Agent.
   American Society of Travel Agents (ASTA)
   1101 King Street, Suite 200
   Alexandria, VA 22314
   Tel: 703-739-2782
   Email: askasta@astahq.com
   http://www.astanet.com

For information regarding the travel industry and certification, contact
Institute of Certified Travel Agents
148 Linden Street, Suite 305
Wellesley, MA 02482
Tel: 800-542-4282
Email: info@thetravelinstitute.com
http://www.icta.com

For information on travel careers in the U.S. government, contact
Society of Government Travel Professionals
6935 Wisconsin Avenue, Suite 200
Bethesda, MD 20815
Tel: 301-654-8595
Email: govtvlmkt@aol.com
http://www.government-travel.org

For general information on the travel industry, contact
Travel Industry Association of America
1100 New York Avenue, NW, Suite 450
Washington, DC 20005
Tel: 202-408-8422
http://www.tia.org

Index

Entries and page numbers in **bold** indicate major treatment of a topic.